Square pegs and round holes

Regardless of our child's learning style or learning needs, there are things we can do to support them.

A lot of parents live in fear that if they attempt to explain something to their child, it will confuse them. But sometimes we need things presented in a different way in order for them to become relevant and make sense to us.

I remember as a child sitting in a GCSE maths class and the teacher was explaining something to us. I had no idea what she was talking about and, unfortunately, she chose me to answer her question.

I sat and looked at her blankly before giving her an answer with only the slightest glimmer of hope that it might be right.

No chance. She explained it again using the exact same words. She asked me again for the answer, but I was none the wiser. She might as well have been talking in a foreign language. I had no clue.

With a roll of her eyes, she explained it for the third time in the exact the same way. I still had no idea what she was on about. But, now with a bright red face and a fear that the tears I could feel welling up inside would escape down my cheeks, she gave up. I felt like a complete fool in front of the whole class.

That night I sat with my dad who used completely different wording and I got it. It was simple. He wasn't a teacher; he just had the patience to explain it to me in a way that I understood it.

That has stayed with me for a long, long time.

Over the coming pages and chapters I want to explain how we can adapt, sometimes in the smallest of ways to make learning maths and English accessible to those who don't fit the round hole created for the education system. As more and more children, for a huge range of reasons seem to be finding themselves shaped more like a square peg and struggling to fit in, discovering that the school environment wasn't designed for their needs.

Many of the techniques and reasons that I have presented are based on the experiences I have encountered over the past 20+ years and are relevant regardless of the label that we are defined by, whether that be mainstream, dyslexic, ASD, ADHD, AD, anxious, etc.

Chapter 1

When we are in a situation when we aren't thinking logically, or our natural way of thinking isn't the linear route that is expected to be the norm, or we are sat in an exam or the teacher just takes it upon themselves to single you out to be the person to answer their question, it is unlikely that our brain will hurry straight to the specific piece of information that we need.

Instead, it starts darting around inside our head like a ping-pong ball looking for that relevant nugget that will save the day. It travels all around the houses, the most scenic route it can possibly find and then often fails to locate that titbit that would have been so appreciated in that moment of time.

When we do something, we create a memory. So, if we ask a child to do a worksheet, they will store that information somewhere in the depths of their brain. To reinforce this information, we ask them to do another worksheet. And maybe another, each time congratulating ourselves on the support we are giving to our child.

However, when the child is asked a question relating to the information on that worksheet, their brain only has that one specific memory where it can find the information.

So instead, if we provide a series of different resources, we are helping them to create multiple memories.

Learning the times tables can give a simple example of this.

If we keep asking our children to recite them by rote, or suddenly bombard them with a general times tables question we are creating 1 memory.

However, if we play a game of bingo, pairs, fishing, noughts and crosses, snakes and ladders with a question focused to one specific times table written in each square, we can provide a range of memories making it easier for the child to recall the information when needed.

Additionally, if we ask the children to write out the times table in advance in a variety of large, bright colours we are opening up additional neuro pathways helping them to create more places in the brain to recall the information. You might choose to use scented pens to take the whole sensory experience up a level!

What's more, the advantage to having the specific times table written down is that, not only will it provide a memory which will be stronger if they have created it themselves, it will also provide them with a check/ cheat sheet, which will offer them the confidence needed to answer the question. Initially, they may use it excessively to find the answers. This is fine because they are learning the correct response. As they become more confident, they will need to rely on the written answers less and less and take pride in not needing to relate to it anymore.

(I've heard of a game where you sit in a circle, and someone throws a ball at you and asks you to answer a random times tables question. For me that would have been the ultimate cruelty as a child having to think about the maths and the co-ordination needed to suddenly catch a ball with no forewarning, so be sure the tasks you use are relevant to the child's idea of enjoyment and ability).

Chapter 2:

How often do you feel inspired to do .
something you really don't want to do?
Something that is outside your comfort zone
and seems irrelevant to this moment in life
anyway.

My suspicion is that you're struggling to think
of an honest answer to that...

That's another reason for trying to make
learning an enjoyable experience. I doubt it
will ever be regarded as light entertainment;
however, it doesn't need to feel like you are
trapped inside the lion's den either with no
means of escape!

When we use games to support our children's
education, we are hopefully making it more
appealing.
In the previous chapter I used times tables as
an example of using games and a variety of
resources to support our child's education. But
that is just one specific area that can be
adjusted to support all forms of education.

The goal is, if we can entice our children in with something more enjoyable than a worksheet, they are more likely to want to participate. We can eliminate the hours of arguing and tears to achieve what should have been a 5-minute task. Success, give yourself a pat on the back.

So, for example, if we offer to have a game of noughts and crosses (with a twist) whilst we wait for the vegetables to boil, the adverts are on, etc they are probably more likely to be drawn in. (I'll explain the noughts and crosses game in a moment).

The more they participate, the more practice they get. With practice comes skill and confidence. With confidence comes the willingness to participate and we suddenly find ourselves in a positive spiral.

Confidence isn't everything, but it is a key factor that holds many people back.
I appreciate that not everyone will agree with what I am about to say but, I'll put it out there anyway.

Very often children who are struggling at school will feel like everyone else is better than them. They are a failure; they can't do it. It's too hard.

When we play games, let them win sometimes. WHAT? Life isn't like that!
I know, but they are children, and they already feel like they have pulled the short straw so occasionally give them a break. Let them feel what it's like to win. To beat a parent or an educator. Let them experience the feeling of doing well and not always being the one who failed, the one who couldn't do it. The one who might as well just quit.

The power of winning from time to time will be such a huge confidence boost. Those few seconds that you shed tears because you lost will mean the world to them, especially if they know how competitive you are.

Noughts and crosses:
This is a game I adapted from my lad, Jamie when he was doing his GCSE's.
Draw 2 horizontal lines and cross them with 2 vertical lines. This forms the grid.

If you are practising the times tables, decide which one you are focusing on and write it beside the grid. Then write a number from 1 to 12 within each square of the grid itself.

Now, like in the traditional game of noughts and crosses you take it in turns to claim a square. The first person to get a row, diagonal, or column of three is the winner.

However, in this version, before you can claim your square you need to multiply the number written there by your chosen times table.
Example: You have decided to focus on the 5x tables.

You want to claim the top left corner in the grid. In that square is the number 2.
Before you can write your nought or cross there, you will need to state the answer to the question; 5x2 which would be 10.

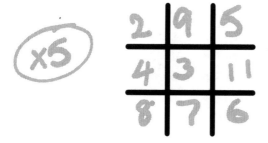

This game can be adapted in many ways, but one way I have found beneficial, and I will quickly mention is when children struggle with writing specific letters or numbers. 'b's and 'd's often prove complicated, as do 'p's and 'q's but we will talk about this more in the dyslexia chapter.

Instead of using noughts and crosses, pick a letter (coincidentally one your child struggles with) and a second letter. One of you will be one letter, the other chooses the other. This time to claim your square, instead of writing a nought or cross, you write your letter. Then swap letters and have another go.

It takes seconds and is far more enjoyable than spending time tracing the shapes of letters in pre-school books and more age appropriate for an older child who struggles.

Something else I am a strong advocate for is starting just below our child's level of confidence.

Something else I am a strong advocate for is starting just below our child's level of confidence.

I'm suspecting that if you are reading this part of the book, it is because you have decided you want to support your child's education. Maybe this is to compliment what they are learning at school, because you home school them, or because you simply enjoy spending time with them. There are probably 100 other reasons why. Regardless...

If there is an area they are struggling with and you agree to focus on initially, start at a level slightly below where they feel comfortable. If for example, you have decided to work on times tables, as they are simple to use for demonstration purposes, and you know your child can do the 10's and 2's but is struggling with the others focus on those 2 initially. (Here is a link for our free times tables e-book that I created a couple of years back that you might find helpful:

https://theclarajamesapproach.co.uk/times-tables-download

Why?

Because then you can boost their confidence by showing them what they can do. You're not suddenly reassuring them that their opinion that this is too hard for them, is right!

Don't run before you can walk.

If it takes you days or weeks to conquer them, don't worry, you will get there in the end. The more practice you put in during these early stages, the more it will pay off in the long run. Reassure them. Offer them praise when they do well. Even if it's only that they get one question right, focus on that one rather than the ones they struggled with, but obviously don't be patronising...

Like I said provide prompts, do what it takes to boost their confidence so that they believe that it is something they are capable of achieving.

Then as they gain confidence in that area, start to slowly introduce the next. Let them know it's because they are now a master of what you've been doing previously that you can move on.

This book isn't meant to be an: "everything I know about educating children and what I know about different types of learning 'difficulties'" so I shall keep this bit short.

However, if you want more support, if you have any questions get in touch or follow us on social media, or maybe join the Clara James Approach our membership group.

(There is a discount code for you at the back of the book).

Maybe you want to work as a tutor with children with SEN, again, get in touch and I promise I will always do my best to help: info@clarajamestutoring.co.uk

This chapter isn't written so that people can diagnose dyslexia themselves at home.
Diagnosis needs to be done by a professional.

Instead, it is written so that if you are a parent or an educator of a child who struggles with aspects of writing, spelling, reading or maths, and you want the tools to support them, this section will help you to do that. Maybe dyslexia is a term you have heard of, or you know very little about it and you want to learn more.

Every page has a wide margin. This is for two reasons:

1. The more the white space area there is on a page, the easier it is to read. (This is something you also need to remember when you are working with a child who struggles to read).

2. As you read through you may find you want to make notes for yourself. These wide margins will give you the space to do that.

What is dyslexia?

Dyslexia is a term that is becoming increasingly common. My goal in this section is to give you an overview as to what it is and how we can support those who are regarded as dyslexic.

Before we begin, can I explain?

Back when my oldest daughter was young, I thought she might be mildly dyslexic. I had been on a course at the local college focused on "supporting reading and spelling difficulties". As part of that course we had to do a case study. I chose Clara.

At the end of the course, the lady running it, suggested I had a word with the school to ask for their advice.

When I approached the school, their response was: "Dyslexia is an excuse for laziness, I don't think you have a problem". End of story.

I didn't have the confidence then to fight my corner, so I decided to learn what I could about different learning styles myself. I hoped that it would compliment my degree and at the same time I could support my daughter.
That was how my interest in the subject began.

The term dyslexia is defined in the Oxford English dictionary as: "A general term for disorders that involve difficulty in learning to read or interpret words, letters, and other symbols, but that do not affect general intelligence."

A more detailed definition is given by the British Dyslexia Association:

• The word 'dyslexia' comes from the Greek and means 'difficulty with words'.

• It is a life-long, usually genetic, inherited condition and affects around 10% of the population.

• Dyslexia occurs in people of all races, backgrounds, and abilities, and varies from person to person: no two people will have the same set of strengths and weaknesses.

• Dyslexia occurs independently of intelligence.

• Dyslexia is really about information processing: dyslexic people may have difficulty processing and remembering information they see and hear. This can affect learning and the acquisition of literacy skills.

• Dyslexia is one of a family of Specific Learning Difficulties. It often co-occurs with related conditions, such as dyspraxia, dyscalculia, and attention deficit disorder (ADD).

• On the plus side, dyslexic people often have strong visual, creative, and problem-solving skills and are prominent among entrepreneurs, inventors, architects, engineers and in the arts and entertainment world.
Many famous and successful people are dyslexic.
Another definition which is worth considering was presented by (Lyon, Shaywitz, & Shaywitz, 2003, p. 2) stating that: "Dyslexia is a specific learning disability that is neurobiological in origin. It is characterized by difficulties with accurate and/or fluent word recognition and by poor spelling and decoding abilities. These difficulties typically result from a deficit in the phonological component of language that is often unexpected in relation to other cognitive abilities and the provision of effective classroom instruction."

Although I want to focus this section on dyslexia, there are other similar difficulties that you should also be aware of as they often go hand in hand and share many similar characteristics,

The characteristics of dyslexia are very similar to those of dyspraxia.

There is no one type of either dyslexia or dyspraxia and it's common for these traits to overlap. Both are described as "Specific Learning Difficulties" and very often one person will experience both.

Whereas Dyslexia is regarded as relating to difficulties with the written language, dyspraxia is more related to the ability to do things (Praxis comes from the Greek word meaning to do).

Dyspraxia is defined as: "Three abilities are required for effective praxis: these are the abilities to conceptualise, organize and execute sequences of unfamiliar actions. If one or more of these is impaired, then dyspraxia may result.

Dyspraxia is also known as Developmental Co-ordination Disorder (DCD) and expresses itself in problems in areas such as adequately recognising; interpreting, organizing, and integrating sensory information to produce an efficient response.

Child dyspraxics are often referred to as having "clumsy child syndrome" due to their tendency to bump into things and they frequently have trouble with sports, for example catching or hitting balls.

Between 5% and 10% of the population are affected." Definition by "The University of Hull - Understanding Dyslexia and Dyspraxia"

Dyscalculia

Again, there is a large amount of overlap between dyslexia, dyspraxia, and dyscalculia. My favourite way of highlighting the similarities is presented by Sheldon Horowitz: Director, LD Resources; National Center for Learning Disabilities.

He recommends you imagine a math's lesson. In this lesson, both those who struggle with dyslexia or dyscalculia will find the language of math's a challenge making it difficult to understand and interpret what the question is asking.

Dysgraphia

Again, this is closely related to dyslexia.

According to the National Center for Learning Disabilities (NCLD), Dysgraphia is a learning disability that affects writing, which requires a complex set of motor and information processing skills.

Put simply, Dysgraphia makes the act of writing difficult.

It can lead to problems with spelling, poor handwriting and putting thoughts on paper. People with dysgraphia can have trouble organizing letters, numbers and words on a line or page making the presentation of the work more difficult.

One of the issues with recognising dyslexia is that it can present itself in many different ways.

Dyslexia is a very general term, and the traits will regularly overlap and will often vary from person to person.

One common problem faced is a difficulty with hearing different sounds.

Some people will prove to be efficient with recognising words they have seen before and practiced using but may well struggle with "reading" out the sounds (phonemes) that create new words.

Phonemes are the individual sounds in a word; for example, cat has three: c/a/t.

"Computer" would be made up of more and obviously therefore, make it much more of a challenge.

Some sounds are harder to hear than others such as 'b' and 'p' as they are both "soft sounds" which are created with a soft "burst of air" when spoken.

Apparently, the easiest way to notice the difference is by touching your voice box as you say each one and you are supposed to feel a slightly stronger movement when you say the letter 'b'. (I haven't noticed this to be the case I must admit!)

There are other similar sounding letters which can add to this confusion. Letters such as:
k, and g.
f and v
t and d

s and z
ch and j
m and n
f and th (th like in the word thin)

Problems of this sort are called "Phonological processing".

Put simply, this means your child would probably struggle with handling of the sounds of individual letters within the words when they speak, listen, or try to remember them.

The processing aspect relates to what your brain has to do in order to try and make sense of it.

One method of recognising if your child has a difficulty with this is to make up rhymes together using words that sound the same at the end such as: like, hike, Mike and bike. Creating rhymes such as: Does Mike like to ride his bike or go on a hike?

We used to make up rhymes to sing to our old dog, Snow: "We all love Snow, she's perfect did you know. She likes to have a rest, because she's the very best!" (Please don't judge!)

A child who struggles with "Phonological Processing" would struggle with the creation of rhymes such as either of these.

These rhymes can be changed so that you are using the same sounds at the beginning of the words.

There are loads of common examples of phrases which could be used here such as: six sizzling sausages or she sells seashells on the seashore.

Not been able to hear the differences in the words could be an indicator, that this is something your child potentially struggles with and needs investigating further.

Not only may sounding these words out cause difficulties when reading, but also pronouncing them may cause some worries.

The biggest problem that could present itself is when trying to spell. If your child can't hear each individual sound in the words, sounding it out will become much more of a problem.

A second difficulty could present itself when someone struggles to remember how both individual letters and words look.

This is known as "Orthographic processing". The term orthographic refers to the letters, numbers and symbols that are used in writing.

Although seeing the letters / words backwards isn't necessarily the issue, getting individual letters and words back to front might be. 'p's and 'q's may become confused for each other and words such as dog and god may become interchanged.

Most people will remember a word once they have read it only a few times, for some dyslexics they may need to reread it many, many more times before they become more confident with it.

I love the idea put forward by Alan M. Hultquist in "What is dyslexia?"

He compares letters to pictures.

He suggests imagining a picture of a dog, it can be sitting, walking, sleeping, jumping, doing anything it is still a dog.

Loves a car ride

No matter which angle you look at a dog, she will always look like a dog. However, many letters change.. Reverse a p and it becomes a q, reverse a d and it becomes a b, etc.

However, letters and numbers can only be presented in one specific way. If they are presented in any other way, they cease to be that letter or number.

This can cause huge problems for some people!

Words with similar spellings but completely different meanings such as they're and their can also be challenging.

People who have this form of dyslexia can usually read and spell fairly confidently providing all the letters in the words match the sounds that they make.

Unfortunately, in the English language there are so many words which cannot be sounded out phonetically, or two words that sound the same can be spelt differently and have completely different meanings such as two, to and too. For and four are other examples of this. The list of possible examples is endless.
You'll find games that can be played to support the learning of these type of words over in the Clara James Approach, but my favourite is probably my version of Pictionary.

You have a list of words which sound the same but have different meanings or spelt the same but sound different (homophones and homographs).

The first person chooses a word from the list but doesn't tell the other person what they have chosen. The first person then draws an image of their chosen word. Person 2 has to try and guess what they are drawing.

Once correctly guessed, you write the word with the correct spelling next to the image. Your artistic skills aren't important, it's the recognition of the correct spelling that is key.

I was playing this with a lad the other day and he drew a wall. I guessed a word. Wrong. Another word. Still wrong. A third attempt and still I was wrong. Finally, I had to ask what the image was of. He explained that he was reading behind the wall!

I'm afraid I didn't get that one. But the game is fun and is a great way to put visual images with the words in a manner that should be fun.

The third form of dyslexia that some people will struggle with is reading and spelling. Reading is often very slow and although they read a word previously in the text, they may have to sound it out again the next time they come across it in a different sentence.

A big issue with reading slowly is that the text may lose its meaning as they can't remember what they have read and sounding out each individual word takes away from the flow of the passage.

A game we often play in the lessons (and again can be found over in the Clara James Approach) is one that I call the dotty board game.

On a sheet of A4 paper make a path of 18 dots. 6 will perhaps be red, 6 might be green, and you might choose yellow for the final 6. Also create 6 forfeits such as miss a go, move forward 3, go back 6, the other person reads, etc and number each one from 1 to 6.

You each choose a colour. For the purposes of this example, I'll be yellow, you can be red. You roll the dice and move the appropriate number of spaces. You must keep going, you can't double back on yourself halfway through a go.

If you land on a yellow, I'll have to read as appropriate. If you land on a red, you'll have to read. Should you land on a green, you roll the dice again the number will determine your forfeit.

You can change the dots to something more relevant to your child's interests if you like.

The purpose of the game is to take the onus away from one person having to do all the reading. It gives them the opportunity to enjoy the story as well.

I know when I was young, if I had to read out loud, I would get in such a state over it that my words would come out as a jumbled mess. By sharing the reading and incorporating it into a game, it hopefully relieves some of the stress and makes it a more enjoyable experience.

Many years ago, I read somewhere, that for many dyslexics, each time they read it is like reading a different foreign language. Remembering the meaning of the symbols and the context of that symbol amongst the other symbols, then remembering what it all relates to, is almost impossible.

The final and probably the most common form of dyslexia is "Mixed Dyslexia".

It is probably the one that most people with dyslexia will show aspects of. Mixed dyslexia is a combination of elements from more than one of the above categories.

Research into dyslexia is ongoing though currently evidence is pointing firmly in the direction genetics.

Studies at the University of Bristol of over 10,000 children born between 1991-1992 identified genetic variants that could increase a child's likelihood of receiving an early diagnosis.

There is also a strong belief that dyslexia is influenced by which side of our brain is dominant. The human brain is complicated and responsible for everything the body does: it controls movement, receives, stores and analyses information.

The brain can be divided into two hemispheres the left-hand side and the right-hand side.

The left-hand side is concerned with tasks such as:

• Sequencing
• Storing facts
• Using language
• Emotions
• Structured activities
• Organisation
• The knowledge of "how"
• Logical reasoning; cause and effect, breaking things down and drawing logical conclusions

The right-hand side has a totally different function. It is concerned with:

- Thinking about things holistically, considering the whole picture
- Working with pictures
- Using visuals (shapes and colours) for explanations
- Using images to help with memory
- Expressing emotions
- Being playful
- Improvising
- Its intuitive

It is commonly believed that those who display dyslexic and dyspraxic tendencies are more likely to be "right brain dominant".

This would make them better at problem solving and thinking outside the box. Where they might show weaknesses in some of the areas controlled by the left-hand side, the right-hand side overcompensates, making these qualities even stronger.

Tell-tale signs/ characteristics associated with dyslexia.

As I Mentioned earlier in the introduction a formal diagnosis would need to be carried out by a qualified professional, however before approaching a professional, you probably want to have an idea of what you are looking for.

Although this is obviously a very basic, generic list, these 10 steps will give you an early indicator of whether it might be worth making more detailed observations and seeking further guidance:

1. Are there other family members who experienced difficulties learning to read or write when they were at school?
2. Is your child reluctant to go to school?
3. Does your child have difficulty with spelling?
4. When reading does your son/ daughter miss out words?
5. Do they have difficulty when reading aloud?
6. Does your child sometimes skip lines when reading aloud?
7. Does he/she experience difficulties when copying from the board?
8. Do they get confused about following instructions (for example when playing a game?)
9. Is your child able to count down from 100 to 0?
10. Is anyone in the family left-handed?

Apparently it is also common for a dyslexic child to move their whole head when reading rather than just using their eyes to follow the line of words.

A quick PS: Before we finish looking at what dyslexia is, I think we ought to consider what dyslexia isn't.

It isn't:
• a lack of motivation,
• a sensory impairment
• inadequate opportunities
• A lack of intelligence

Chapter 3

When I was researching for my book "Essential guide to supporting Parents and Tutors ..." I asked a friend who is dyslexic what she felt was important to include and for her, it was the fact that dyslexia impacts on every aspect of your life in so many ways.

Possibly the main effect dyslexia will have on people will be on their self-esteem; the knowledge that they seem to struggle in areas that other people seem to find so easy.

In the previous chapter, I tried to highlight that the brain of someone with dyslexia works differently from another person's brain. As a consequence, some things that most people take for granted are suddenly much more difficult to accomplish.

For instance, copying something down from the board in class: Most children will glance up, acknowledge what needs to copied, then put pen to paper and write it down. They may need to glance up once or twice more to clarify, but it is a fairly painless task. Yet, for the dyslexic child, the task may seem considerably more complex.

As you can imagine, for children with dyslexia, reading is a huge struggle. Words which seem easy such as: a, the, or and, can create huge problems.

A relatively simple sentence such as: "A black dog ate a bone and a brown dog watched." The more complex looking words such as black and watched can be visualised and are therefore easier to read, unlike the words which most people would deem to be easy such as; a, the, or, etc.

From fairly early on in a child's education a child is expected to do a certain amount of comprehension; answering questions about a piece of text that they have read. This skill is then built on and follows them throughout their entire academic life.

There are several skills required in being a fluent reader:

·   As you know, the alphabet is made up of a series of different symbols called letters.
To be able to read it is essential that the child can recognise that every symbol/letter represents a certain sound.

However, some letter combinations may cause the letters to make different sounds such as a c and h together now create the sound made by a train or at the beginning of the word chair.

These sounds are referred to in schools as phonics. It is by recognising these sounds that the child has the ability to sound out a word.
· Once the child can "decode" each individual sound in each individual word and string them together to make a word, they will then be able to start reading sentences.
· As the child becomes more confident with this, they will be able to recognize words at a glance. They will, in theory, no longer need to sound out each letter. Most children perhaps need to see a word a dozen times before they recognize it, for a dyslexic child this could take considerably longer.

· As a child becomes more fluent, their reading will pick up speed and the words will flow more smoothly.

· Once you can read the text fluently you can then start to focus on the content which will support their comprehension skills.

Above I have highlighted five basic skills required in becoming confident enough at reading to develop their comprehension skills.

For dyslexics, the art of reading is considerably more challenging.

Recently, whilst researching for this book, I found an explanation, which I love and feel, explains the difficulties perfectly.

If you look at a picture of a dog drawn from any angle it will always be recognisable as a dog.

However, if you draw a letter or a group of letters from various angles it will no longer represent that letter. Let me give you an example: a p drawn upside down becomes a d, a u drawn upside down becomes an n. (What is dyslexia; A.M.Hultquist 2010 p .36), where as a dog remains a dog...

Although not every dyslexic child may see letters differently, they may struggle to remember the difference between similar letters.

For some people, the challenge may be that the letters 'move' or 'vibrate' on the page. But the biggest problem faced is there is no sense of connection between individual letters and sounds.

Nouns (things) may be easier to remember as a visual image can be associated with the letters helping to secure their meaning.

Another issue is that one sound can be written in several ways. A prime example of this is with the k/c/ck. King, cat and tick all make the same sound yet written in three different ways.

Then, to complicate matters further, letters can have several sounds: snow (the white stuff that falls from the sky on a cold day) or cow (the farm animal that gives us milk).

Then the letter order will also affect the meaning of the word: saw has a completely different meaning to was, or angle has a completely different meaning to angel.

Clearly, the problems are numerous:

1, If the words are moving about on the page, you need to hold them still otherwise keeping your place and deciphering what the letter says will be a nearly impossible task.

1. Then, recognizing what each individual sound makes and establishing what sound it is supposed to make for this particular occasion when placed with other letters.

2. Recognizing that the order of the letters will change the meaning of the word.

3. Then whilst holding this word in your memory move on to decode what the next word means, and what the one after that says so that you can string together this information and ultimately give it some meaning!

I would suggest that you take your share of the reading so that your child has the opportunity to enjoy the text as well. If they are reading and struggling over a word, help them.

The longer they struggle trying to work out what the word is, the more likely they will forget everything else they have previously read, and the text will lose its meaning.

Remember that reading is exhausting!

Consider everything your child must do, just to read one word. Don't expect them to read for long periods. Keep it short and snappy and perhaps incorporate it into a game, such as the dotty board game?

Spelling

Another issue faced by dyslexic children is their spelling.

Having read the above section it becomes easier to understand why, especially when you add to this the fact that in the English language one out of 6 words is spelt irregularly, (it can't be sounded out phonetically).

Learning the rules may not always help either as the rules very often need to be adapted.

Make learning spellings fun and relevant. Remember that the more systems you can use to help your child recall the spelling of the words, the more likely it is that they will be able to recall them later.

Be creative and ensure it's active rather than a passive, uninspiring activity. (Suggestions can be found in the Clara James Approach or follow the Clara James Approach Facebook page for inspiration).

Handwriting

The next closely related problem comes from handwriting.

Sometimes poor handwriting skills will be used as a cover up for poor spelling or other problems. I think we are probably all guilty of not knowing how to spell something, so we just scribble it and hope that people presume we have spelt it properly.

"The Gift of Dyslexia; RD Davis, 2010" presents the idea that dyslexics use different neuropathways creating "distorted perceptions".

Because of this, they can't see the straight lines in the letters resulting in inaccurate images in their letter / symbol formations and as a consequence producing illegible handwriting.

Maths

Sequencing is a major issue for most dyslexics because they see things as a whole, rather than segmented into a neat, ordered structure.

Maths though involves a lot of reliance on both time and sequencing and without these two skills, it becomes nearly impossible.

Until the concepts of sequencing and order can be conquered, even basics like counting will remain challenging.

Another issue faced in maths is that the questions are often too wordy.
Not only do you need to decipher what the question says, you then have to establish what it is they are asking you before even starting to think about solving the problem.

Times Tables provide the foundations of all maths and although they can be the ultimate challenge it's worth the effort. There's no rush.

Even if it takes months to cement one of the times tables, it will be worth it.

I will offer some suggestions on games you can use later on in this book.

A commonly known problem for those with dyslexia is their poor memory skills.

I was recently speaking to someone who is dyslexic, and he was telling me about his gap year in Australia. I said it must have been an amazing experience and were abouts had he been.

Sadly, he didn't know, he couldn't remember the names of the places. He knew he had travelled up the east coast but could remember no more detail than that...

Yet some things that those with dyslexia can remember are incredible. The smallest details of things they have personally done or experienced, or information that is embedded in a story or humor. This information may often be remembered far quicker by them than that of a non-dyslexic person. But impersonal, abstract information escapes them.

This can cause problems with exams as educational systems are inclined to treat intellectual information as the only type of information that is relevant. To make the situation worse, information is normally taught in a passive manner.

If these abstract facts cannot be memorized, then the candidate is seen as not knowing and marked accordingly.

Poor memory skills can also create problems with timekeeping and organization.

Organization can be a huge issue when trying to file things away. The ability to see something in a more holistic way means that something can be filed under a number of categories.

Because of this it is often easier not to file things but to instead create piles of paperwork where it can be found more easily.

Remembering what things: books, PE kits, etc. are needed on specific days for specific lessons may also prove to be a nightmare.
With time and time keeping also causing difficulties, getting to lessons on time can also be a huge issue.

Clumsiness

Another problem which people are often less likely to be familiar with is clumsiness. We will discuss later an ability to see the bigger picture and recognize unusual connections.

This clumsiness often causes additional problems with precision, accuracy and never conquering the clumsiness that is commonly associated with toddlers.

College

Finally, as a person progresses through the educational system, they will experience an increasing amount of emphasis on reading and writing and a greater standard of written work will be expected.

For any child leaving home to attend higher education, it is a traumatic time but these additional difficulties will heighten the pressure even further.

I don't want to dwell on the doom and gloom of being a dyslexic because many people have used their dyslexic traits to their advantage.
Some people have used the traits which distinguish them as being dyslexic, to massively succeeded.

The number of successful dyslexic people is astonishing. The areas in which they succeed are also greatly varied.

I could list people here who have succeeded despite their dyslexia, or maybe because of their dyslexia, but the list could spread over pages.

What I suggest is that if there is an area you or your child are interested in, research that specific area. Find relevant people in that field.

Perhaps it is business that interests you in which case you will probably come across people like Sir Alan Sugar, Richard Branson or even Steve Jobs the founder of Apple.

Maybe it is the world of film that fascinates you.

Here you will discover people such as Jennifer Aniston: the actress, producer and businesswoman who came to worldwide fame for her part as Rachel Green in the American sitcom Friends. Alongside her are others such as Anthony Hopkins, Tom Cruise, Kiera Knightly or Danny Glover.

Many of these people have written about their experiences and how having dyslexia has moulded them.

Celebrate the achievement of these people and use them as role models to others who feel that their dyslexia has placed restrictions on what they will be able to achieve in life.

Dyslexia: the Gift

Dyslexia presents itself in many different forms; consequently, the gifts that people experience also come in many different forms. Unfortunately, dyslexia is often seen as a disability, which concerning certain academic tasks it clearly is, however this is only one part of it and there is a very clear flipside.

Spatial reasoning

Spatial reasoning is a huge strength experienced by many dyslexics. This involves the ability to look at shapes, positioning, size, and direction and see how they interact.

Children displaying strengths such as these may be drawn to construction toys in their younger years such as building bricks. Any artwork they produce could demonstrate a multi-dimensional or 3d perspective.

Research suggests that these special talents are inborn rather than achieved through experience and practice.

These childhood past times have occasionally proven to influence the type of work that a child with these talents will excel at in later in life. Examples of jobs might include architecture or engineering.

Relationships

It has been suggested that some dyslexic authors have built their success because of their ability to make complicated connections between events, recognising patterns in sequences. Providing more superior, intriguing plots.

Many dyslexics also show an amazing talent at recalling past personal experiences and using them to explain present or future events.

Evidence has been provided that suggests that although the short-term working memory may prove to be problematic for many dyslexics, their long term (which can be subdivided into the declarative memory (which stores facts about the world) and the Episodic memory (which stores personal facts and experiences), is incredibly effective.

It is this episodic memory, which is held responsible for understanding the present and creating predictions for the future, which is held responsible for demonstrating formidable skills in novel writing.

This ability to recognise relationships possibly stems from how a dyslexic person accesses the information in their memory.
One metaphor (The Dyslexic Advantage: Brocke, Eide & Eide, pg 116) describes the memories of an event in a person's life stored away after the performance in a warehouse. When these memories are needed you just pop back to the warehouse to find them.
This metaphor is then expanded using the idea that when information is needed, you can scroll through these articles (visual images in the brain) to find the necessary information giving access to more creative and complex ideas and suggestions.

Predictions

We mentioned the skills of making creative predictions about the future and how this compliments the art of novel writing and storytelling.
This skill can be expanded further. Many dyslexics also have the ability to accurately predict what will happen in the real world by using best fit scenarios.

By using non-verbal reasoning skills, mathematical and symbolic clues, they can piece together events and create a fairly accurate hypothesis as to the direction that future events will occur.

By using this range of skills it is far more beneficial than looking at statistical data that would be provided by a preprogramed computer/robot.

Talents such as this are a blessing in the world of entrepreneurial-ship and science, where making predictions to the outcome of a set of reactions is invaluable.

Examples might include how will the market will respond to an event, the introduction of a new service/ product. Or, how would tweaking something in a scientific experiment have an effect on the final outcome?

In the world of business where things are constantly changing and are often unclear, this ability to see the bigger picture and piece together fairly accurate predictions is invaluable. It often stems from a curious personality, why does this happen, what happens if this happens; the young child who always answers a statement with a question and always has to ask why!

Key skills of the dyslexic entrepreneur

A sense of vision for their business

A confident and persistent attitude (if you can survive school and the modern-day academic system you can survive anything)!
A willingness and ability to ask for help and to find helpers who are better than yourself at the required skill.

They possess excellent communications skills and the ability to inspire your staff.

A strong sense of intuition

One dyslexic was quoted as saying that the problems you face in school create these characteristics in you in order to survive and succeed in an environment which is so "prejudiced" (my choice of word) against you and the way you think and learn.

I don't want to dwell on these for too long as the purpose of this book is to assist you when working with children and adults who show dyslexic tendencies.
However, you do need to be aware that dyslexia is not just a disability; it is also the means of experiencing many great strengths which are not attainable to the majority.

Chapter 3

When I set about writing the original course which this book is based upon, I asked what people would like to see included in it. I hope this unit will answer most of the responses I received.

Please remember that a diagnosis needs to be done by a professional, these following points are predominate to guide you in deciding whether an assessment should be considered.

My child struggles at school; do you think they could be dyslexic?

There are some issues that will accompany a dyslexic person through life and can often be spotted from a young age. These might vary between "good" days and "bad" days though there may not be any obvious reason why. Determining what is meant by instructions such as;
in/out, up/down, forwards/backwards.

Sequencing, as mentioned previously can be problematic: counting, reciting the alphabet, days of the week. Another pointer to consider is a family history of dyslexia or difficulties at school.

From as young as pre-school there may be indicators. Tasks that most children find both easy and fun will be a challenge such as learning nursery rhymes and coming up with rhyming words such as: three, tree, see.

Everyday items may be wrongly labelled such as a leaf may be used when describing a feather and sometimes words may be persistently jumbled up such as "pea tot" for tea pot. Each of these points relates to speech difficulties, and in many cases, speech may come late to a dyslexic child.

Other non-verbal indicators may also be evident such difficulties with getting dressed: putting shoes onto the incorrect feet. Some dyslexic children may never crawl instead they may shuffle around on their bottoms or their stomachs.

Although a young dyslexic child may show enthusiasm at being read to, they will typically show little enthusiasm in either letter or words and will often be accused of not listening or paying attention.

A young dyslexic child may appear to be excessively clumsy, walking into things and falling over. Tasks such as catching, throwing, or kicking a ball may also prove to be far from easy.

As the child moves into formal schooling more difficulties will start to reveal themselves. The most likely will be difficulty with reading and spelling and when it comes to writing some symbols may be presented backwards or the wrong way round (as spoken about previously). Sometimes letters will be left out of words, or the words will contain the right letters but be presented in the wrong order. Written work will take longer to produce for a dyslexic child than for other children in the class.

Learning times tables, the alphabet, and other sequences such as the days of the week and months of the year continue to be far from easy.

Even simple calculations need to be made with the support of their fingers or other aids such as marks on a piece of paper, counters, etc.

Reading will be painfully slow and processing what they have read will cause further problems.

Critically, concentration will appear to cause problems.

The non-language indicators continue and become more pronounced as the child gets older. The difficulties with dressing and tying shoelaces continue along with recognising their left from their right. A lack of confidence and a meagre self-image is also evident. Yet the child who is displaying these signs is also amazingly bright and alert in many other aspects.

As the child gets older the indicators become more apparent. The above indicators remain in evidence. But in addition, by the time the child reaches secondary school their reading has not improved and their spelling is still causing difficulties.

Instructions with more than just one or two steps cause problems because of their short-term working memory, remembering telephone numbers also causes issues (though these days that is less of an issue as they can simply be programmed into most telephones). Remembering times, places and dates also create issues which may appear as if the child is disorganised or forgetful.

Pronouncing long words again is problematic. There is an increasing amount of recognition that speech disorders and stumbling over the spoken word have a link to dyslexia.

Writing and planning essays and long pieces of work again creates great difficulties.

As the child progresses into adulthood this poor confidence and lack of self-esteem remains a paramount issue in their lives. Yet contrary to this the areas of strength that they possess that we considered in the earlier unit, will start to become more and more evident.

If you are concerned about your child, it is always worth asking. If nothing else, it will put your mind at peace.

If they are in school, ask to speak to their class teacher or the school's SENCo as your first port of call.

What age can I get an assessment for my child?

Every child will progress at different rates, so primary schools and other academic institutions are often reluctant to get a child assessed at an early age.

Consequently, it is often as the child reaches the later years of primary school or secondary school that a formal assessment might be suggested.

However, as soon as your child is showing signs of struggling or if your child is showing signs of distress or showing behavioural issues an assessment should be considered.

If it is deemed that additional help is needed, the earlier it can be put in place, the better the outcome will be for your child.

Can I get an assessment done at my school?

Some schools will offer a basic screening test. Although it might signpost some dyslexic tendencies it is unlikely to be a reliable full test.
At the time of writing this, a full dyslexia test can be requested. The cost will vary from £300 upwards. It will need to be done by a Specialist Dyslexia Assessor with a current practising Certificate.

In the UK, a list of qualified assessors can be accessed through the British Dyslexia Association.

What does a test involve?

These tests will cover three key areas:

1.   Key literacy and numeracy skills such as reading, writing, spelling, and arithmetic.

2. Language, memory, and processing skills that are known to be closely linked to dyslexia. This is key as they aspects are what are normally recognised as the largest barriers to learning.

3.   General language/ reasoning and problem-solving skills.

These are important for several reasons:
It will highlight the discrepancy between a person's ability to explain things verbally, compared to when they are asked to write it down with pen and paper.

It will also assist with helping to recognise if there are any other barriers to learning or, just as importantly the test will also highlight any strengths that can be developed and used to help find methods of compensating for some of the other areas of weakness.

What help will my child be offered in school if they are recognised as being dyslexic?

This is very much at the discretion of each individual school. Generally speaking, the school will look at the difficulties experienced by the individual child and will put in place support deemed necessary.

For some it may be up to 13 ½ hours a week intervention. Sometimes they may offer 'dyslexia friendly interventions' though please be aware this will vary greatly from school to school, and county to county.

The budget the school will be able to access to support your child will be based on a formula which is agreed between the school and the local authority.

Schools are obliged to "use their best endeavours" for children with additional educational needs. OFSTED will also be responsible for establishing how well children with SEN are learning, and how much progress they are making with their schoolwork.

After an initial review with parents, schools are responsible for both identifying and ensuring suitable requirements are reached for your child.

The reviews should take place fairly regularly so that suitable support can be provided.

The reviews are regularly monitored because:
Your child's needs may change.

The school acquires new information about your child's needs.

For The requirements will potentially change as your child's needs are met and they reach their targets.

New evidence arises about their progress.

The school may receive new information on how to better support your child's needs.

Discussions with yourselves or other caregivers reveal that different tactics may be better suited to your individual child.

If the local authority wants to change the provision that your child is receiving, they may request an annual review to discuss this. (If there isn't going to be a review, ask for a meeting to clarify why they want to change the support that your child is receiving).

The thing I would recommend most strongly is to find out who the SENCo is for the school and talk openly and honestly with them about your concerns.

Most SENCo's want to help and you're insights as the parent are invaluable to them. Try to build a bond with them so you can work together in the best interests of your child.

How can I help my dyslexic child/the child that I work with?

Confidence is key!

However, something else which has been highlighted repeatedly is the issue with organisation.

There are a few practical ways you can easily help with this.

Firstly, I would help the child prepare a time table so that he has a record of where he/she has to be and when.

More than one copy may be beneficial: one at home for when they are organising their bag/homework for the next day. One to keep in their pocket so they have easy access to a reminder of where they need to go to next and if practical a class timetable could be put up in the classroom.

Try to be discrete with this, as they get older it is unlikely that they would like everyone to know it is there for their benefit. The timetable may be illustrated if this makes life easier and could also contain a map highlighting where each lesson will take place.

The next step that could be taken is to colour code each book so that at a glance the child can see that for English they need to take all the books with a green sticker on.

This again could be linked back to the timetable: for example, a simple red spot in the corner of the timetable or perhaps the writing for English could be done in a corresponding green.

Ask the child if they would like your support in keeping their books and belongings organised as dyslexics are renowned for loosing things.

Although this may seem like a mammoth task initially, it will make their lives considerably easier.

When researching for this book, I read an article that highlighted that dyslexic people will often create piles of things rather than filing stuff away as they can see so many logical places to file it, therefore it seems easier not to file it.

Try to encourage them out of this habit because although it may (in the short term) seem like the easy option, it is very time consuming trying to locate things at a later date and also very frustrating for other people.

Although I'm not dyslexic, this habit of creating piles of work rather than filing stuff away is a bad habit of mine, one I have tried to overcome but so far am failing miserably in the process. I know life would be so much easier, more organised, less time consuming if I didn't just create piles of things around the place...

Take one category (maybe their homework) and work on getting that organised, once that's proving successful try to work on something else. Don't try to do everything at once and work together on it, that way you can incorporate what actually works best for your child, rather than what we think would work best for them/ what works best for you.

If time keeping is an issue, give them prompts about how long they have. For example, if they have 5 minutes before the end of the lesson, point this out and give it something to compare to: "You have 5 minutes left, that's about as long as the adverts last when you're watching..."

The over-riding support you can give is to ask them the help they would appreciate and how they would like to be helped.

Don't be judgemental, just reassure them that if they want your help, you're there to support them the best you can.

When setting tasks make sure they are achievable when considering the outcome and also will they be able to concentrate long enough to complete the task.

Remember that dyslexic children will find some of these tasks far more tiring because of the additional effort they will need to put into it.

Is there a certain time of the day that they feel most tired? Is there some way that they can discretely have a rest and reenergize?

Would a study buddy be of benefit (peer support) or would they rather work alone at their own pace? If you do find a study buddy for them, make sure it is someone they are happy with and not just someone that you as an adult would consider to be suitable.

When the child has got free time available to them, make sure that activities are available that they enjoy and reflect their strengths. Building on their strengths in one area will help boost confidence and their self-esteem across the board.

Teach logic rather than by rote.

If you are teaching something through logic it is more likely to make sense and they will be more likely to make a connection with it. If, however, you teach by rote it will make no sense.

I was talking to a local business person about how times tables used to be taught by rote. He was telling me the scenario/joke: A teacher asks a child to recite a particular times table. The child replies; "der der du der" The teacher asks them what they are doing. The child replies they can remember the tune but not the words.

Although it was meant as a joke, I felt there was actually an awful lot of truth in this, reciting a long sequence of numbers that has no meaning will be very easily forgotten.

If they have something concrete to visualise, they are more likely to understand that, for example, 5 groups of 4 puppies would equal 20 puppies and this is exactly the same as 5x4.

I won't get into too much depth here as it will be covered in more depth in the supporting maths chapter, but I want you to be aware that something with meaning is a lot easier to learn than anything else.

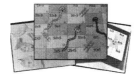

This Chapter will be relatively short, but I feel it is a necessary one as a connection between the theoretical units of the previous three and the more practical units of those still to come. At times in this chapter I will talk about learning words and sounds as examples so it is easier to explain myself.

If we want to support a child with their learning, we will need to do it in a way that is effective for them.

For example, it wouldn't be beneficial for them if they learn best by looking and watching, if you sat and talked to them for a period of time.

Equally it would be counterproductive to show them something if they were audio learners.
Keynote: Talk to the child and involve them when considering the best way to teach them and what learning style will best suit their needs. Remember this throughout as it will be one of the biggest benefits you can offer the child.

There are four ways in which a person can learn (learning styles).

These are visual, audio, tactile and kinaesthetic experiences, which will provide memories for the child to recall when needed.

Regardless of what the child's learning style is, if you can expose them to a variety of experiences and learning styles within each activity, they will be more likely to recall the information at a later date.

Each time we do something we create a memory in our brain. When we need to recall this information, our brain looks for those memories making the information available to us. Therefore, the more memories we produce when learning something the more likely it is we will be able to recall the information when required.

Typically, in classroom situations a teacher/lecturer will talk to the class on a given subject. This may be followed up with a group discussion and completed with a written task of some description.

For a dyslexic child, this will be insufficient; they need a more interactive route into learning like those used by the kinaesthetic learner; using all five senses if possible. No dyslexic child will be able to thrive until they have determined what their ideal learning style is.

Examples here could include:

If we are trying to support a child with their times tables, something that often proves difficult, we could have a pairs game, the fishing game. A game of snakes & ladders, a colouring challenge. Putting smarties, grapes, etc into groups of that particular amount and working out how many there are in specific numbers of groups and relating that to the given times table.

By using multiple resources, we create multiple memories and use multiple senses, making it easier to find that nugget of information when needed, instead of it being just out of reach in the back of your mind/ on the tip of your tongue.

A visual memory is created when a child creates a memory from something they have seen.

They do not need to interact with it on a deeper level. Examples of this would include pictures and images around the house, school, environment. If you are supporting your child with letter recognition, anywhere where a picture is shown next to the letter sound so that the child is able to make that visual association would serve as a visual memory.

There are numerous examples of environmental print; words and numbers are found in endless places within the western world:

Calendars, catalogues, menus, time-tables for buses and trains, newspapers, TV guides.
Audio Memories:

An audio memory is created when a child creates a memory from something they have heard.

This can be in the form of been told on the TV, radio, music, in a conversation or something or by hearing themselves say something.

Audio memories are particularly effective when it is their own voice they are hearing; consequently, getting the child to say it themselves will be more effective than listening to someone else telling them.

If the child is shown something at the same time as they are told about it, they will potentially start to build up an association between the two.

Tactile memories:
A tactile memory is made when a child creates a memory from something they have felt. This can be created by using such resources as clay, play dough, plastic, or pipe cleaners.
It can also be created by your child feeling a shape which has been glued onto a piece of paper using sand, string, or sandpaper, etc.
An advantage to these is that the child can be involved in creating the letter sounds themselves.
For instance, making a letter shape out of pipe cleaners is a simple, mess-free activity.

Children should initially be taught the lower-case letters when doing this.

Kinaesthetic memories:

A kinaesthetic memory is created when a child creates a memory from something they interacted with.

Examples of this include games, crafts, etc.

Children normally enjoy these activities, which is important, because if children are enjoying themselves and are in a relaxed state, they are more susceptible to learning.

Kinaesthetic memories can also be created through activities such as air writing, ie - writing the letters in the air on a large scale.

Alternatively, this can be done on large sheets of paper or with water and a paintbrush on an outside wall on a nice day.

Creating actions associated to each sound is also effective. The more personal and relevant to their life, they are, the more effective they will be.

Hence the more of these sensory activities you can introduce to your child, the more likely they are to make multisensory memories and be able to recall them in the future.

These learning styles also link to learning components; again, there are four of these:

Information Input: the methods and techniques we use to absorb information.

Information Output: this refers to the techniques and systems we us to communicate information with others.

Memory: This is key to recognising our ideal learning style.

We talked about memory earlier in chapter 1, and how it is divided into long term and short-term memories.

Our short-term memory is where we store current information that can be easily accessed.

This long-term memory can also be subdivided into procedural and factual memory.

The procedural memory helps us to recall rules and rote tasks so that they can be performed without too much conscious effort. Factual memories can also be subdivided into personal (learned through personal experiences; this is often the favoured long term memory style of a dyslexic person as it provides something they can relate to a specific experience) and impersonal experiences (also known as semantic or impersonal memories which are more abstract.

Attention: This is something that many people with dyslexia or ADHD struggle with.
When someone has a fairly small working memory, they will often find they will find it difficult to maintain their attention. This is because their working memory is being overwhelmed hindering their ability to maintain their focus on a task over a long period of time.
Attention is influenced by factors such as motivation and interest in the subject being taught.

Again, regardless of the child's learning style, it is important to teach things in small manageable chunks, if too much is presented in one go the odds are that they will tune out.

It is better to set very small targets, reach them, ensure a proper understanding, then move on. If the foundations are not strong the rest will crumble and there is a lot of truth in the phrase: "Don't try to run before you can walk".

As I have previously stated, it is important that the child is relaxed, and enjoying themselves, so that they are more likely to recall the information when required in the future. Consequently, if and when possible, incorporate these activities into games, crafts or other less formal 'academic' activities.

Anyone who is recognised as being dyslexic will undoubtedly have a great level of intelligence. It will be their short-term and long-term memories which will let them down.
Because of their advanced intelligence it is possible to rely on their knowledge of the English language to learn spellings rather than learning words through rote. Something

learned through rote will have no meaning and will mean learning each word individually. Give everything logic and they will find things far easier to grasp.

A leading British Psychologist, Dr Angela Fawcett, recommends a system entitled the "the procedural learning system".

The concept behind this system is about learning how to learn, and learning something to the point that it becomes automatic, and you no longer need to think about it.

This is the part of the book I've been looking forward to writing. I hope you find it helpful.

Supporting Writing

Before I start there is something that I need to point out and will reiterate several times over the coming pages:

Always find a reason to congratulate and praise the child.

This will help boost their confidence and self-esteem and with this their enthusiasm to take part and learn.

However, it is equally important that any praise given must be genuine. If you offer praise when something hasn't gone well acknowledge the fact it hasn't gone well, but you are sure with work they will achieve it, or maybe it was just an off day and the next time you try, things will be more successful. Somethings will always take longer to learn than others, but you were really impressed with the effort that they put into it, and you appreciate that maybe they probably found that frustrating.

Well done for trying to stick it out...

I know it's easier said than done sometimes, but always remain positive and if things are plummeting downhill at a rate of knots, have a break and come back to it with a fresh look on things.

Writing needs to be carried out automatically so that letters can be formed neatly and consistently.

For children who can't manage to perform the task automatically, it will be significantly more difficult.

Writing is an incredibly important aspect of our lives. Teachers will often request a handwritten response to a question in a test, forms, job applications.

Writing can be made considerably easier with proper instruction. It should be recommended that learning reading and writing should be worked at together, as each one will complement the progress of the other.

The method of writing starts with the following sequence:

1.Putting pen to paper to form individual letters and then words.

2.Once the ability to write individual words has been achieved, sentences can be tackled
.
3.Once sentences have been mastered, we can move on to paragraphs.

4.Paragraphs will then lead us on to writing full essays, stories, or reports.

The teaching methods must be interactive. Learning is much harder when they are expected to be passive learners. Being proactive with the learning will also help keep them motivated and will help make the activity more fun.

Work with your child's strengths. This will help them make progress and achieve targets set. Work with them to set their own targets, allow them to be independent learners. Allow them to write for themselves if and when possible, this will also help with self-esteem and confidence.

Many different and interesting reasons for writing need to be offered to help make the experience more enjoyable.

As a rule of thumb when putting pen to paper it is generally recommended that a dyslexic child learns cursive writing.

Because of the dyslexic child's struggle with 2 dimensional spaces, they will often struggle with where to start each letter. Cursive handwriting will help to counteract this problem as all the letters are joined with just gaps between the words.

Yet talking about cursive writing to most children just makes them want to pull their hair out with frustration. Forming individual letters, though theoretically harder, still seems to be preferred.

With the pencil moving from left to right to form the words, it again helps the child with their spatial awareness and the direction which the words should take.

However, contrary to this some argue that because it is different to the text they see in books, etc. it will prove to be confusing though there is no firm evidence of this.

Other children, and parents, also say their writing is even harder to read when they try to join the letters.

If problems with handwriting persist it may be worth seeking the help of an occupational therapist for an evaluation.

Writing letters

Before we can write words, we need to be able to write individual letters.

In my honest opinion, the worse place to start with this would be with writing small formal letters on a piece of A4 paper. Not only is it a repetitive and mundane task, but it also requires a lot of concentration.

We need to create activities which are enjoyable and relaxed.

Make it large: Start by practising with the large muscles. This can be done in several ways.

Use larger sheets of paper and dedicate just one or two letters to each page.

Depending on their ability you may wish to start with simple circles, waves, and lines.

Letters are placed in groups, those which involve a swing upwards: i, j, p, r, s, t, u, and w.

Those letters which require loops: b, e, f, h, k and l.

The up and over family: m, n, v, x, y and z. Finally, there is the around-up family which include the final set of letters, a, c, d, g, q, o.

Practising loops, waves and lines will support the child when writing the actual letters. Don't restrict the activity to using just writing pens, use paint, chalk, felt tips, anything you can think of to make the activity more enjoyable and memorable.

Alternatively, if the weather permits, take a bucket of water and paint brush and create the letters as large as you can on the footpath or the side of a building. The water will evaporate, and any mistakes will evaporate with it. If something is done with success and you want to keep a record of it, photograph it before it's gone.

A sandpit or beach is another fantastic place for practising writing letters. Again, they can be created on a far larger scale and any mistakes can be eradicated with no formal or lasting record.

Different materials: Don't get hung up on the idea that writing needs to be done with a pen and paper.

On a piece of paper write the alphabet in upper case (capitals) in chronological order. Then working together, or asking your child to work independently, use either clay or a similar substance, to copy and create the letters. This is great for several reasons:

1.You are using a variety of different skills to achieve this which will create a range of memories and make recall easier as required.
2.For most people, getting your hands messy and being creative is an enjoyable task.

3.Earlier it was discussed how dyslexic people can visualise something from more than one angle. Letters on a piece of paper have to be seen from one angle. By making a physical impression of each letter, it will help anchor the shape down and make it more "concrete" in its appearance in the child's mind.

Once they are left to harden off, they could be painted decorated in a range of colours/styles to help make each letter an individual.

A similar technique can be used with pipe-cleaners though this is not as easy as they are harder to mould into accurate shapes. Once each upper-case letter has been mastered, move on to the lowercase.

Write the alphabet out in its entirety so that it can be copied in a systematic order?
Once the letters have been accomplished, you can have a go at numbers.

White boards are another great use as, once again any mistakes can be removed with no permanent record whereas work which the child is proud of can be photographed and kept as a record of their efforts.

It is good to keep some records of early efforts as these can be shown to the child to show them the progress that they have made over the course of the lessons.

When you come to forming actual letters, talk your child through every step of producing every letter. Remember there is no rush and each step should be taken slowly. Once your child is fairly confident with the steps, ask them to talk you through how you produce the letter.

Some dyslexic children will struggle with "mirror writing" writing letters back to front, upside down, etc. Examples of this include creating a b instead of a d, a p instead of a q or a b instead of a p.

There are many methods to support a child with this for b's and d's in particular:

1.Write the word bed. Consider the sticks at the end of each letter as a bedhead; it helps give the letters a concrete image.

2.This same idea can be used by putting your hands into fists with your thumbs sticking up and out. Your left thumb is the b as that comes first in the alphabet and in the word bed. Your right thumb is the d because it comes second in the alphabet and in the word bed.

3.Create collages of words, letters or pictures of things starting with either a b or d. Use various sources and textures to make it as interesting and memorable as possible.

Provide the child with a cheat sheet reminding them how every letter of the alphabet is formed so that they can refer to it whenever they feel the need.

As we learn how to write each letter, we will need to learn the sound each one resembles. However, once your child is familiar with these blends and confident with writing letters it is easy to progress onto words.

We can practice this through writing words using scrabble letters, the pipe cleaner and clay letters we produced earlier. Magnetic letters that we cover our fridges with when our children are little or any other letters of this type.

When you are working with your child, work as a role model. Participate in the activities as well, work as a team although you will need to guide and be the team leader. Offer words that the child can copy.

As you would suspect, these words can slowly be built up into sentences and from here much longer pieces of writing.

Writing reports, essays, and other longer pieces

Once you move on to writing longer pieces it is important that you give your child templates that they can use to help structure their work.

Examples of completed articles can also be used to give them ideas which they can model their own work against.

As before, creating the document verbally before putting pen to paper may be of benefit.

When writing, a dyslexic child may struggle with starting new sentences and knowing what content and specific words to put into it. If this happens stop writing and brainstorm ideas. Offer prompts and use their individual interests to help with offering ideas.

Again, I often find it beneficial to have word banks of adjectives (describe the object, person, thing) or adverbs (describe the doing word) that they can refer to help with extending their language. They can also use this to offer ideas for words and help with spelling.

Mind maps, sketches, doodles, diagrams, and so on, can all be used when coming up with ideas.

Initially whilst practising longer pieces of writing, stick to topics that the child is interested in and knows about to help them make a flowing piece of writing.

As many as half the dyslexic children who make it to college will struggle with the rules of grammar.

When you start to look at grammar, keep it simple. Restrict the amount of information that you offer them in each lesson.

Make sure the initial rules are ones that can easily be incorporated into their work.
As always keep it fun and use games which incorporate a range of techniques and multimedia.

Before concerning yourself too much with the grammatical rules, work on the content that they are writing rather than the structure.

Don't rush with putting pen to paper, use oral practice first so that the child is confident about what needs to go into a sentence. This will then be one less thing to worry about when moving on to putting it down on paper.
Once this is in place the main basic concepts your child needs to know and understand are:
A noun is a person, place or object and an adjective is a word to describe the noun.

A verb is a doing word, and an adverb describes the verb.

A sentence must include a subject (who or what the sentence is about) and what is happening to the subject.

Every sentence starts with a capital letter.
Every sentence will finish with a punctuation mark.

There are terms such as pronouns, conjunctions, prepositions, and articles in the English language that your child needs to understand and be aware of.

They need to be aware of where different punctuation is used and that commas help create a pause when speaking.

Encourage them to edit their work for themselves. If someone else takes it away to correct and type up, the child loses ownership of the work.

If someone else corrects the work and hands it back, it reinforces the child's self-image that they are not very good with writing.

Learning the ability to self-edit will be an empowering task and when carried out on a regular basis will help the child correct their own mistakes, boosting confidence and self-esteem.

Spellings

The underlying goal for both reading and spelling is to master phonics (Phonics are the sounds that are created by individual letters and letter blends), recognising rhymes and the effect that changing the form of a word can have on the meaning of the word.

An example of this could be sing, sang and singing. The biggest problem with spelling words using the English language is that the set of rules you are given to support you with this task often doesn't apply as there are many irregular words to learn, approximately 85 of the words in the English language are irregular!

Again, rely on your dyslexic child's high intelligence and logical thinking and use this logic when you are teaching them spellings. Offer motivation and support.

Also, offer chances to relax. This will not only help with their motivation but also their memories as they are less likely to suffer a mental overload.

The first thing you will need to establish is, does your child recognise the individual letter sounds of the alphabet?

Offer them a piece of paper with the numbers 1 to 24 on it. Ask them to give you a number between 1 and 24. You will hold a piece of paper with the following letters written on it:

d
m
k (as in cat)
t
s (as in sit)
l
g (as in game)
w
h
j (as in jam)
b
kw (q)
f
z (as in zip)
r
j (as in giant, g would be the answer you are looking for here)
ks (x)
n
s (as in city)
y
k (as in kite)
v
z (as in is here the answer is s)
p

Ask them to write down the letter that you give them next to each appropriate number.

For some, you will need to offer the letter then a word that that particular letter starts with: c as in cat.

Not only are you checking how many answers they get correct but also how confident they are with the task.

Once you have completed this you will need to move on and check how well they get on with the vowel sounds.

If the child demonstrates a lack of confidence at all, don't rush ahead use a variety of multisensory tasks to build up their confidence.

Multisensory tasks and games you could use: Pairs: matching a picture of an object to the letter that it starts with for example matching a picture of a dog to the letter d.

Collages: like recommended earlier, find pictures and words starting with the appropriate letter. Use textured letters as well. These could be made into a scrap book or posters that can be displayed around the room.

Draw the noughts and crosses' grid. Inside each square draw a picture starting with one of the letters they were struggling with.

Before you can claim your square, you have to say what letter that particular picture starts with.

Alternatively, you could draw the grid, then in order to claim your square, you each take on one of the challenging letters and use that to mark your square instead of using a nought or cross.

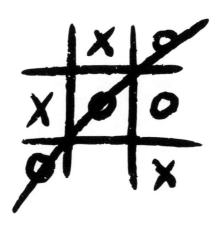

Create a bingo board for each player. On each board draw a picture in each square starting with one of the sounds that they are finding difficult. Then create a set of individual cards with a letter on each.

(Each letter will associate to each picture; you may have a card with a picture of a cat on, you would then have a corresponding card with the letter c on). The first person to cover their board is the winner.

Please remember that the aim of these games is to boost the child's confidence. It may be beneficial to allow your child to win the game from time to time.

We have got templates for many of these games in our membership group, and new activities are added each month. There are more details and a special offer at the back of the book.

How is the English language structured?

The problem with the English language is that there are so many rules to learn about how it is structured. Once you have mastered these rules, you are then confronted with the fact that, there are areas where these rules don't actually apply.

However, the following points will give you a basic overview of the structure used.

The English language is made up from 21 consonants. These sounds normally end quickly such as p, t, or m.

There are a number of consonants that are blended together to create a unique sound, these include ch, sh, ph, and th.

Additionally, there are also a number of vowels which blend together to create a unique set of sounds. This list includes the oo in moon.

Then comes a mixture of consonants and vowels. This list could include: ble such as the bul sound at the end of table.

Next, we move on to units of sounds called syllables these have at least one vowel.

Closed syllables are a single vowel which is followed (and completes the sound) by a consonant. Examples of this would be words like: it, cat or dog.

Vowel-consonant-e. This is sometimes referred to as the magic e and is one of the hardest syllables to learn. When you use this syllable pattern the e makes the vowel softer and longer. Examples of this would include words such as: fine, cone or same.

Open syllable: These syllables take a vowel and do not follow it with a consonant, so when you say it your mouth remains open. Examples would include words such as: no, me, ski.

Vowel combination syllables: This is when two vowels are combined together to create one sound. Examples include the ee in tree or the ai in plain.

Consonant-le syllable: This is a less common blend and is only used in multi-syllabic words. It will be made up with a consonant such as b or d and will offer words such as handle or syllable.

R-controlled syllable: The letter r seems to dominate any vowel that it follows, almost drowning it out. An example of this is the 'a' in car can't be heard instead you are just aware of the c and the r.

Word endings also have a set of rulesassociated with them.

The 'e' rule: when a suffix (word ending such as ly, ment, ing) which starts with a vowel is added to a word that ends in an 'e' the 'e' is dropped. An example of this would include words such as flake would become flaking, joke would become joker.

The doubling rule: When a suffix that starts with a vowel is added to the end of a word which ends with a single vowel then a single consonant, that consonant will be doubled. Examples of this rule could include run = running, jog = jogger or jogging

The Y rule: When a suffix is added to a word that ends in a Y this is changed into an i if the y would be followed by a consonant. Examples of this would include funny would become funnier or happy would become happiness.

Two important generalisations:

ss, ff, ll spelling generalisation: if a one syllable word ends in a single s,f, and has a single short vowel, double the last letter. Examples include: huff, stuff, press, hill, chill.

ck generalisation: If a k comes directly after a short vowel at the end of the word it changes to ck. Examples of this could include clock, sock, flick, chick.

If you are planning on working on spellings with your child keep it structured and predictable as this will offer the reassurance that they won't be asked to do something they're not capable of doing.

Always remember to work at their pace and offer plenty of reassurance. Explain at the start what you are going to be doing.

Talk about and review what you covered previously.

When you come to moving on to a new letter say to them a few words with this letter in.

If you were moving on to the vowel sound e, you may say: egg, beg, fed, red, bed, ted and ten. Then ask if they could hear a similar sound throughout the words. If they get it right, offer praise, if they can't spot it, write the words down and see if they can spot it then.

Again, offer the praise as necessary. If not, tell them not to worry and tell them what the sound is that you'll be working on.

Ask the child to write the words down for themselves using a pencil but with a good quality rubber to hand so they can correct it if necessary.

Use wide lined paper. Self-editing as mentioned before is of great importance because of how it will boost their self-esteem as they come to recognise their own mistakes.

As your child becomes more confident with the word, ask them to write it in context, if relevant maybe even illustrate the sentence.

Before asking them to do this, write the sentences to show them how it should look first. If there any words they are unsure how to spell give them the spelling, use your instincts on the best way to do this; guide or give.

Once they've completed editing the work for themselves, ask if you can have a look. If you spot any mistakes, put a small, discrete mark next to it. Then ask them if they can spot the word on the line that needs to be changed.

As before, there is no rush in moving on. Move too slowly rather than too quickly. Play a range of games for reinforcing the spelling of each word.

In this modern day and age, some of the pressure can be taken off with the use of technology. Encourage the child to use spell checks for basic spellings but be aware that they may not yet be able to spot homophones, words which are spelt differently but sound the same, such as plane or plain, draw or drawer.

Homophones

Homophones are words which sound alike but have different meanings: too, to, two, their, there, they're, are possibly the most commonly used in the English language.

When you start working on these with your child, introduce them with caution as they are particularly difficult. Only introduce them once they are confident with all the above rules and only as a side project to the usual learning.

Make it enjoyable.

Two games I use when introducing homophones include:

Which witch?

Have a list of words written down on a piece of paper:

Blue / blew
Rain/ reign
Called / cold
Flower / flour
Ball/ bowl
Letter (alphabet)/ letter (that you would post)
Bat (cricket) / bat (animal
Hour / our
To / too / two
Eight / ate
Plane / plane
You / ewe
Which / witch
Their /there/ they're
Piece/ peace
Draw / drawer

The above are just a few examples, you can probably think of others.

Take it in turns to pick a word.

Don't tell the other person which word you have chosen.

Try and draw a picture associated with the word.

Don't worry about creating artistic master pieces, the game is aiming to give each word a visual memory and bringing an element of enjoyment to the task.

Once the drawing is finished, the other person must try and guess what it is you have drawn. Once they have guessed, the "artist" has to write the word (in a sentence if you deem that to be suitable) next to the picture.

Snakes and ladders

On a piece of paper draw a board, roughly 6 squares by 4. On most of the squares write a homophone.

Then draw in approximately 3 snakes and 3 ladders.

As you move around the board you climb the ladders and slide down the snakes as you might in the traditional game.

However, if you land on a word you need to put it into a relevant sentence (either written or spoken). The first one to the finish line is the winner.

(Again, templates for these can be found over in the Clara James Approach membership group).

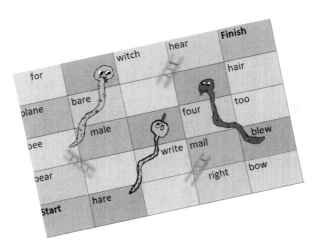

Maths is obviously a huge subject, so I won't be able to go into how to support each subject within maths. Instead, what we will look at is supporting maths in general.

For some children, Maths is unbelievably hard and the difficulties they face in maths seem to be endless.

It can be hard for any number of reasons.

Before children start school, most children will (although often unknowingly) have their first experiences with maths; they will see numbers, shapes, sizes, colours, patterns and sequences in the world around them.

This is just the tip of the iceberg for their experiences and as they progress into school these experiences will multiply, and most children will begin to notice these patterns and similarities and start to make important connections. Unfortunately, though, some children won't make this life-altering connection.

Although Dyscalculia (a neurological difficulty with calculation) is fairly rare, many dyslexics do struggle with many aspects of math and very often both of these traits very closely co-inside. These difficulties can vary greatly but will quite possibly include any combination of the following:

·   Remembering simple sequences such as which order numbers go in, the days of the week or month or harder ones such as times tables.
·   The language used in maths.
·   The physical act of writing of numbers and other symbols.
·   The issues involved with copying from the board or other places.
·   Spatial skills required when calculating longer, more complex problems.
·   Recognising simple patterns.
·   Estimating.
·   Correctly using your left and right.
·   Memory problems with remembering mathematical facts.
·   Knowing where numbers on a clock go and reading what time the clock is telling you.
·   Visualising mathematical concepts as much of it is presented in a two-dimensional fashion.
·   Interchanging the order of numbers:217 could easily 712 or 172, etc.

These issues are made worse by the challenge or sometimes inability to transfer skills learned in one subject to those needed in another.

Sadly, sometimes these issues then start to create a fear of maths which then leads to anxiety and a loss of self-esteem.

Confidence plummets and here starts a self-fulfilling prophecy of failure.

This is why (and I will in no doubt repeat this many times more) I believe we must offer justifiable praise even for the smallest thing so that we can try hard and boost their confidence.

As pointed out before though, there are some very gifted dyslexic mathematicians such as Albert Einstein.

It is suggested that the figure is probably close to something like 1 in 10 dyslexics will excel in maths. But it is vital that for this to happen the right support is given from an early age.

The right support will always need to be tailored to the needs of that specific individual child; a one style suits all approach just will not work.

The best way to establish what your child needs is to talk to them; they know themselves best.

Do mnemonics help them, colour coding, games, computer work, listening, drawing, writing, experimenting, any of, none of, or all the above?

Many of the suggestions made here on how to support a dyslexic child with maths will co-inside very closely with the ones made in the spelling and writing section.

When you're working with your child, use concepts which are concrete and make sure you spend a lot of learning time with them. Always make sure that this time spent is relaxed and enjoyable for both yourself and especially your child.

If you look bored, fed-up, uninspired it's not going to motivate them to want to participate.

Start with working on single concepts. Always work at the pace of your child and don't feel you need to rush. The main priority is to get these foundations firmly in place, without them, everything else will crumble.

Once these foundations are secure and your child is confident with them you can then; and only then, move on to looking at topics as a whole. From here you will be able to move on to more advanced work.

Remember, never to rush. It is better to spend too long on something, than rush through it and still not really understand it.

Many children will not reach their full potential in maths until long after they have left full-time education and it will be life skills and experiences which will teach them most successfully.

Initially, keep everything as 3 dimensional as possible using physical aids to help whenever possible. When you do move onto 2-dimensional resources start with pictures, then finally abstract symbols such as numbers, signs, and equations.

Use active learning, encourage your child to experiment with physical objects and inspire them to talk about what they are doing and what they are learning.

Some children who are struggling will find confidence from talking to other children who are struggling. It's moral boosting to know you are not alone in your struggles, they can also share techniques that have worked for them and in helping others support their self-confidence.

When working with your dyslexic child work as a team; motivate each other, help each other, and support each other. Most parents want to do their best for their child. But then you worry that you don't understand the methods used in schools. this often then translates into a reluctance to help in case you do the wrong thing.

At some time, most children will express a fear of a certain aspect of maths and will live in dread of the day!

To try and counteract this, set small targets which are easily achieved. Celebrate when each and everyone is achieved and again never move on too quickly. As said before, slower is better.

For some people, one issue with maths is that it is a precise subject and follows a firm set of rules. There is only one right answer. This could give the mindset that there is a higher chance of failure as it is harder to bluff your way through.

Schools seem to embrace mental maths tests which, repeatedly tests all those skills dyslexic children fear and have yet to conquer.

This often reinforces the feeling of inadequacy and failure.

Present new concepts chronologically and each time you're working together make sure you review what you've done, what you've achieved and if there is anything you want to spend some more time doing.

When you start the next lesson, again recap what you did last time and how this will connect to it.

Use the physical environment around you to help with understanding mathematical concepts: size, quantity, do things match?
Is there a recurring pattern of shapes, colours, or sizes?

Go out into the local environment to learn. Real-life hands-on experiences will make learning much more relevant and make the logic to it easier to grasp.

This again avoids lessons being taught by rote and logic will be easier to apply.

Have discussions on a subject as talking about something often helps with understanding but keep them light-hearted and ensure there is a good working bond between yourself and your child.

As this 'working' relationship grows your child will find it easier to discuss problems they are having in maths and other subjects that they are studying.

Support them with the help they need and again, ensure this help is tailored to meet the areas they want to work on and in a way that is suitable to their specific learning style.

If you want to research this area further, books by Dr Maria Montessori (A Montessori Handbook, "Dr Montessori's own Handbook") and Stern, Stern and Gould (Structural Arithmetic) would be two beneficial books to read. Structural Arithmetic provides ideas on how to support basic addition, subtraction, multiplying and division and although it is primarily aimed at younger children it can be adapted to suit most age groups.

When working with older children, check that they thoroughly understand the basic principles and not just getting by.

If the foundations aren't secure the rest will always be a struggle, as with anything you need a firm base to build anything on or it will crumble.

Encourage your child to experiment with methods and don't let it be a problem if they get something wrong.

A survey showed that children in Japan are actively encouraged to experiment and learn from the mistakes they make, in some circumstances working on something for several hours until they had cracked it. Through this trial-and-error method, the child discovered the logic and systems for themselves and it reinforced their understanding.

Offer guidance and don't let them get too frustrated but this process has proven to create far more competent and effective learners.

By encouraging your child to learn new systems/facts through the practical trial and error method it will make it more concrete and prevent it from being something they experienced through rote learning.

It will also prevent it from being learned in isolation to anything else.

Learning like this will also help place the new knowledge into the long-term memory rather than holding it in the short-term memory.

Research has shown that most children can hold up to 9 pieces of information in their short-term memory. For a child with dyslexia, this may be as little as half. If they can only hold a maximum of 5 pieces of information in their short-term memory, they will struggle to remember very much.

In order to help with memory problems, we can offer:

·   More time,
·   Ensure the language which is being used is understood,
·   Give information in relevant chunks,
·   A personal checklist,
·   Make learning fun!
·   Give clear instructions one at a time.
·   Memory cards,
·   Use colours, patterns, music, discussions, and any other learning technique which will make the learning more concrete and give it greater value.

Present mathematical facts visually rather than by counting by this I mean give the child 3 objects and then an additional 2. How many have I given you in total? (Make sure this doesn't come across as patronising though).

Rather than just counting on 2 more from 3 as this is more likely to lead to the same errors experienced as when trying to learn something by rote.

Encourage your child to experiment with different materials to help them develop their logical reasoning skills.

Whilst doing this encourage them to express what they are doing verbally. This will help them retain the information and clarify their understanding and allow you to discreetly monitor their understanding.

Try to make learning Maths as fun as possible. The more any child enjoys it, the more enthusiastic they will be to participate and learn. They will be less tense and consequently be in a better mindset to absorb the information.

Games

Any of the games I'm going to suggest can be mixed and matched and used with multiplying, dividing, adding, subtraction, naming shapes, counting and so on. (Again, templates and more ideas can be found over in the Clara James Approach membership group).

Snakes and ladders:

We talked about this game previously.
Create the board as you did last time: divide the paper into roughly 6 squares by 4. Then in each square write a question appropriate to what you are learning about.
As you land on a square you need to answer the question written on it (any aids you feel necessary can be used to support your child).
The first person to the finish is the winner.

Noughts and crosses:
Draw a noughts' and crosses' grid: 2 horizontal lines with 2 vertical lines cutting through them. In each block write a question, before you are allowed to claim the square with a nought or cross you must answer the sum written there.
The first person to get a row of 3 wins.

Fishing game:

I love this game; it has always been my favourite! It's quite time consuming to make though.

For each question you are going to ask, cut out 2 fish. (If you are doing the 5x table you would probably cut out 24 fish).

On half of the fish write a sum/question.

On the second half of the fish write a corresponding answer.

Cut each fish out, then

Once they are cut out use a hole punch to put a hole in each one (make this resemble the eye).

Pass a paperclip through the hole.

Next you will need a short stick (I normally use half an old felt-tip pen that no longer works) a magnet, some string and some tape.

Use the tape to attach one end of the string to one end of the pen.

Tape the magnet to the other end of the string.

Spread all the fish out onto the floor with the questions / answers facing downwards.

Take it in turns to fish out two fish (the magnet will stick to the paper clip, use this to pick the fish up off the floor)

If you have a corresponding pair (for example a question and the appropriate answer: 3x5, 15) you would keep the pair and have another go.

The person with the most pairs at the end wins.

Pairs:

Like the fishing game, the purpose of this game is to match a corresponding question and answer.

Again, if you are doing a multiplication set of cards you would have 24 cards. On the first card you would write the first question, eg. 1x5, on the next card write the answer. On the next card would be the next question and so on. Turn them all face down and take it in turns to pick up two cards.

If you pick up a corresponding question and answer you win the pair and have another go. The person with the most pairs at the end will be the winner.

Please remember the purpose here is to build the child's confidence and self-esteem. If they are used to losing against their peers, please don't always to be in a hurry to beat them at home every time as well. Being able to beat you from time to time, will be a great ego boost and will help keep them motivated and enthusiastic.

The language of maths

The language used in maths nearly always proves to be problematic.
If reading is a difficulty in other subjects that will follow into their maths lessons. Often, they will encounter even more difficult words to read and spell.
To make matters worse, the question often can't be solved until you have understood what is being asked. If they are unable to read and interpret the question, there is no way your child will reach the correct answer.
Long questions often also result in more problems.

If the child does manage to read the question, they will often find that they have forgotten what was said at the beginning of the question.

Another issue that will sometimes arise is if a child has issues with reading from left to right, they may not notice a vertical table suddenly appearing in the text. So, when a question is asked about it at the end, it may come as a complete surprise to them that it was actually there!

As a child reaches secondary school, and different lessons are taught by different members of staff, it is quite possible that a maths teacher may be oblivious to a child's reading issues in English. Teachers and parents must talk to each other to support the child as much as possible. As always, remember to listen to what the child has to say.

Another area where children may find issues is with the number of homophones in the English language. Homophones are words with more than one meaning. An example of this includes the word right. It could mean:

Yes, you're right!
Turn right (the opposite of left)
Write something down (different spelling but sounds the same)
Right angle (90-degree angle)
I feel all right (fine)

Another problem arises when we recognise one sign can be referred to in several ways. An example of this is the + sign. Just some of the names it can be named include:

- Addition
- Plus
- And
- Combine
- Join
- Increase

We can help our children by talking about the words and symbols they encounter. At times, it is beneficial to read the question for them. Talk to them about what it is asking, do they understand all the words, all the terminology used. What sort of question is it asking: add, subtract, multiply, or divide? Do they have any idea about how they could set about solving it?

Make flash cards with/for them like a mini personal glossary. Ask them to illustrate any terms they feel would benefit from a visual image to reinforce the meaning of the word. Talk in advance about any phrases/words they may come across whilst studying for a particular area of maths.

Some children always seem loath to write anything down, but this is to be discouraged. There are many benefits to writing down the working out.

When you write things down you can develop your confidence and independence. It gives you the opportunity to show/explain your understanding to others and more importantly, if they make a mistake, you can go back through the working out and see where the mistake was made. Was it a lack of understanding, or that something is written down or calculated wrongly?

Another issue which commonly occurs with maths is in the English language we are taught to read from left to right. Then we get to reading large numbers in maths and we need to start at the right and break the number down into chunks of 3 digits putting a comma

between each chunk. This makes the number far easier to read:
42567319

If this is broken down into chunks, we now have:

42, 567, 319
This can now be simply read as 42 million, 567 thousand and 319.

Again, encourage them to talk about this. The more willing they appear to talk, the more likely it is that they understand what they are doing.

Where and how to start

1.Addition: simple 2-digit problems with no regrouping
2.Subtraction: again use 2-digit problems with no regrouping
3.Multiplication: simple 2-digit problems with no regrouping
4.Division: provide very simple division problems
5.Figure out if it is asking for addition or subtraction (worded problems) keep the actual problem very simple.

1. Finally, figure out if the question is asking a multiplication or division question. Again, this will be a worded problem which needs to be kept very simple.

Allow your child to use aids if necessary to help solve any problems. Always praise anything which is achieved.

Moving on

Once your child has conquered the basics:
·   Counting objects
·   Counting in 10's
·   Finding individual numbers on a number line
·   Counting up to higher numbers
·   Number bonds to 10
·   Using patterns
·   Doubling numbers and other basic addition facts
·   Subtraction
·   Multiplication using multiples and step counting
·   Division using the inverse (opposite) of multiplication

You'll need to move on to patterns, graphs, averages, decimals, fractions, percentages. It would be best to follow a formal program.

There are several to choose from and your decision should be based on whether you want the child to:

·   Visualise and verbalise their ideas,
·   Create mental pictures in their mind,
·   Use worksheets but with layouts that still manageable,
·   Or for the older or more advanced child. There are a wealth of resources available in many different formats and at a range of prices.

When you use physical aids there are no rules to abide by: buttons, blocks, cuddly toys, paper clips and so on are all equally effective. What is important is that it is age appropriate and that there is only one variable at a time.

For example, if you are using bricks for an addition sum make sure they are all the same size, colour etc.

What you may choose to do is 3 red blocks + 2 blue blocks would equal 5 blocks in total. This would make it easy to visualise the separate groups.

Alternatively, you may choose to do 3 big blocks + 2 small blocks (make sure there is a significant difference between the large and the small bricks) but make sure everything else is the same.

Everyday maths

The easiest way to learn maths is to experience it.

Most dyslexic children will be practical people and will benefit from putting it into practice: cooking, volume, pricing, time, timetables, estimating, counting or numbers in the environment.

The opportunities to experience everyday maths are endless; they can also be quick, easy, and within reach.

Calculators

Calculators are great, and they provide quick answers, but mistakes are easily made, so a rough estimation would be necessary. However, this could be problematic. Nothing can compensate for knowing the facts, systems and understanding through trial and error, and appropriate learning.

Worksheets

I'm a huge advocate for trying to avoid worksheets when possible. If it is essential to use them ensure your child has someone at hand to support and assist them.

Also remember to keep the number of questions on a sheet to a minimum.
It would probably be beneficial to cover up any other questions on the page apart from the one you are working on so that they form less of a distraction. You may even find verbally recording the questions for the child to listen to as they read along with a written copy if this helps them.

If you are reliant on worksheets, make them yourself so that they are appropriate to the individual needs of your child. That way you can base it on what is relevant to them. Ultimately, make sure that it is something they can succeed at.

Make sure the worksheet isn't too cluttered. Make it easy to establish what it is that needs doing. Initially, keep it simple with only a few questions. As they get used to the area you are working on you can slowly start to increase the difficulty and number of questions asked.

Parents should encourage their child to relax after school, recharge their batteries and de-stress. Chat to them about their learning strengths and help them to stay calm. Ultimately the parent needs to support their child.

I had a conversation with a parent the other day. She admitted she was a pushy parent. But sometimes I think it is important to remember that if we push too hard, who or what we are pushing will fall. We need to be there to hold them up and support them. Not be the cause of their fall.

Try to ensure that your child uses a homework diary. It may be necessary to ask the teacher to give a printed-out version of the homework so that it's not written down incorrectly.

Also try and assist your child to make sure they are taking the right equipment to school each day.

Help them practice and reinforce basic concepts.
Keep them motivated and any learning that is done at home, FUN!

Like another parent said to me, at the end of the day, nothing is more important than your relationship. Don't let anything ruin that.

It is suggested that 1 in 5 adults are illiterate, to the extent that they wouldn't be able to fill in a cheque.
An inability to read will have endless impacts on a person's life not just academically but also socially and emotionally.

Even in basic everyday existence, hurdles will be encountered that most people would take for granted - reading street signs, instructions on a packet, instructions for playing games or operating new equipment, reading an invitation, menus... and the list goes on.

Many children have already learned to loathe reading long before they get the diagnosis as being dyslexic. There is a strong chance that they will try to evade reading by using avoidance techniques such as starting a conversation about something, needing the toilet, finding something else in the room as a distraction etc.

This is in part because they can't find a connection between the sounds the letters make and the actual letter. This problem is emphasised when you consider that in the English language one sound can be made in several ways: f/ph or c/k/ck.

These sounds (phonetics = the smallest sound in the English language) cause problems for most people with dyslexia and consequently help will normally be needed. Children with dyslexia will struggle to remember which sound goes with which letter. Breaking a word down into sounds or recognising how many sounds are in a word can be a real issue.

From here they are expected to establish when a letter sound should be blended into syllables or words. The complexity of a task that should be easy gets greater by the moment.

Many years ago, someone suggested to me that, for a dyslexic child, each time you try to read something it is like trying to read a piece of text in a foreign language that you have no knowledge of and that has its own alphabet such as Arabic or Chinese.

If you are aware of this, the challenge that a dyslexic child faces becomes more understandable.

In the previous chapter, it was mentioned that the order of digits can rearrange themselves. Letters in words can do the same thing:

God can become dog,
saw can become was,
two can become tow, and so on.

This happens because they simply may not see the difference between the letters or the order of the letters. Again, a weak short-term memory will exacerbate the challenge.

Some dyslexic children may be able to recognise words in different contexts, though their reading will probably be slow and laborious.

This could be because although a child can recognise an individual word in isolation, yet they don't have the skill required to combine more than one word, this is possibly due to the struggle of tracking words along a line. They will possibly appear to float and move about on a page. This then creates problems later with comprehension.

In recent years it has been recommended that various fonts are beneficial for the dyslexic learner as they are easier to read.

One has been introduced recently is called Dyslexie Font which has been created by a Dutch University student who is himself dyslexic. The idea behind it is by altering each individual letter very slightly it makes it harder for the brain to reflect it, rotate it and alter its appearance.

Colour overlays, coloured ink or typing on coloured paper are suggestions that people feel help "hold the letters still on the page". Keeping the amount of writing on a page to a minimum keeps it less cluttered, causing fewer distractions and makes reading easier. However, how reading should be taught is a matter of controversy. Some suggest that children should be taught the phonics. From here, words, sentences, paragraphs can be built upon a basic foundation (a similar philosophy to learning basic facts in maths before going on to using them).

The other side of the argument suggests that words should be learned with meaning rather than a series of linked sounds. My opinion is that a combination of both approaches will be of most benefit to your child.

Fluency is the speed and accuracy with which a person reads and only really comes with excessive reading practice.

This could prove to be a battle!

However, if you can keep them engaged, motivated and enthusiastic this may be easier.

Never set targets too high as you will alienate them, and they will once again shy away from it. Instead, set expectations relatively low so that targets can be met.

This will boost confidence and enthusiasm. Find books that your child finds interesting and relate to the child's level of intelligence, this may be streets away from their reading level, so bare this in mind and choose books with caution.

Obviously, the best subject content should be chosen by the child themselves, as they have the best knowledge as to what they enjoy and what they can manage.

One of the basic facts to remember is that if you teach the child the sound of the letter, they will find it far easier to translate the individual sounds into words.

An example of this is cat.

If it's sounded out using the names it would be:
See, ay, tee

This clearly isn't recognisable as a word.
If, however, you sound it out using the sounds: c-a-t it suddenly sounds like the word you are trying to translate. Letter names shouldn't be considered for a long while yet.

In order to support learning these individual sounds, make the letter physically from clay or pipe-cleaners. Write them in the sand. Make scrapbooks with pages filled with pictures/words starting with the same sound. When you're writing it, write it as big as possible, use different colours for each letter and have fun with it.

Think of words that start with the same sound and make silly rhymes using them; obvious ones may include: six sizzling sausages or Mary might make muffins.

Many dyslexic children will struggle to hear these individual sounds so bear with them whilst they become confident and learn them.

Remember once again, motivation and encouraging the child's enthusiasm is paramount. Keep it fun and stay calm even when you feel like pulling your hair out.

I was reading a blog post from a dyslexic person the other day that highlighted the fact that "a normal person" wouldn't do something they couldn't do; they would just turn their back on it. (For example, I have no co-ordination skills what's so ever, so I avoid ball games at all costs. Yet a dyslexic person is being asked / demanded all the time to do things that they find challenging.

Once the child is happy that they know the names and sounds of each individual letter, start looking at simple cvc words (consonant, vowel, consonant).
Games I use to do this include:

Pairs

Create a set of cards (probably about a dozen). One set will have a word, possibly starting with a sound that you will have been concentrating on, the other set will have a corresponding picture.

You both take it in turns to pick up two cards. If you pick up a matching pair, you keep these and have another go. If they don't match, place them back down and the other person has a go. You may prefer to play it with 2 sets of identical words to match rather than matching a picture and a word.

The board game or snakes and ladders

Create a playing board which is roughly 6 squares by 5. If you're playing snakes and ladders, write a word on each. If you are playing the board game, write a simple forfeit on some such as miss ago, have another turn, go back 3 spaces, etc. and words on the rest of the squares. Draw in your snakes and ladders if appropriate.
As you move around the board, you must read the word that you land on. Guide the child as necessary. Don't rush them and offer praise when necessary.

Slowly as the child becomes more confident you will be able to move on to reading words and sentences. Don't rush this, you have started to build their confidence and you don't want to knock it out of them again...

Probably the best place to start is again with games such as pairs. You may choose not to turn them over, just use it as a matching game. One card might state: The Fat Cat. The corresponding card might have a picture of a ridiculously fat cat on it. You need to match up the two corresponding cards.

This could also be done by having 2 columns on a piece of paper with the picture and the sentences muddled up. Again, you need to draw lines to match them back up.

Recognising print in the environment is another great way to practice. Not only will it help make letters and words more familiar, but they can also be seen in various places and contexts.

Help and encourage as much as is needed. With all these games: Practice, practice, practice is what's key.

The more they practice and get better, the more confident they will become.
The more confident they become the more willing they will be to try new challenges and progress...

But progression must be done at the speed of the child, not the pace the supporting adult sees as acceptable and never compare one child's ability to that of another, we are all good at different things.

That's what makes us all individuals.
When you start formal reading with your child, audio books are a godsend.

Not only will this offer them access to a whole range of books, but if they are familiar to hearing the text before they try to read it for themselves, it will remove some of the fear.

Also allow your child to "read" a written copy of the text alongside the audio version (or yourself) as this will offer confidence.

It's a bit like when a toddler takes their few steps, you may hold their hand and you will definitely be there to catch them.

The same applies here with reading. Boost and support a child's confidence every step of the way. In relation to everything you do this will probably have the biggest effect.

The 'Dotty Board Game'

I have played this many times and it has (nearly) always been a hit.

Choose a theme that the child enjoys such as football. On a piece of paper draw or stick 6 footballs, 6 goal posts and 6 whistles in random order.

Place most around the edge and the remaining few across the centre. This is your board. Choose who will be the goal, who will be the goal posts and the whistle is a safe space.

You roll the dice and move the given number of spaces. Each picture is a space. You can move in any direction, but you can't change direction mid throw. If anybody lands on a goal post, the person who chose the goal post reads a short section of the book. If someone lands on the football, the same applies and if someone lands on the whistle, you're safe. No one has to read.

I've recently found using simple joke books quite affective as the amount of reading required is only minimal and they are generally enjoyable in their content.

Comprehension

This is defined in the Oxford English Dictionary as

"The setting of questions on a set text to test understanding, as a school exercise: [as modifier]: comprehension exercises"

Tasks such as this require the child to not only understand the meaning of a singular word, but also the meaning of that word in the context of other words within a sentence and a paragraph, considering that sentence structure, genre, punctuation can all effect the meaning of a word.

Many children struggle with comprehension. For non-dyslexic children the issues normally arise with trying to understand what is meant by the passage or with attention issues.

However, the dyslexic children will often find understanding the text fairly straight forward but will struggle with decoding the individual words. An easy solution to this is to allow the child to listen to the text.

When this is offered as an option, dyslexic children are often incredibly good at comprehension as they can see the bigger picture and notice the ironies, metaphors, humor and symbolism that is often missed by so many.

As with anything, ensure the child is motivated. Try and focus on texts that the child will find enjoyable: be it stories; crime, romance, science fiction, or life stories, or some other form of factual book based on a subject which they are interested in.

Spend time discussing the main themes in the text, the characters, and other important details. Use mind maps or illustrations to make notes on the characters. Make illustrations of the main settings in the book so that it is both more interesting, and long lengths of writing can be avoided too. Discuss what has happened and why the author perhaps opened the book, chapter, or paragraph in such a fashion or predict what might happen next.

Ask the reader questions and encourage them to ask questions in return. Perhaps make a quiz for each other on the text, this way you can assess their understanding and it will be more relaxed than a formal test/assessment.

Over in the membership group, there are a selection of tasks associated with some books which can be used. The idea is after a short number of pages there will be a task to do associated with what you have read.
It may be a word search, to draw the scene that you have read. To write a diary entry from the perspective of the character, etc.

This way it breaks the text up and offers more interesting ways of asking questions and assessing their understanding than generic worksheets.

I hope this section on dyslexia has proven both helpful and informative and will aid you in assisting your child.

Next, we will move on to supporting a child with ASD, Autistic Spectrum Disorder.

Autistic Spectrum Disorder, ASD

This is one of the hardest things I have had to create as every child you meet with ASD, will be like the rest of us, a truly unique individual. This is key, don't get bogged down with the label, consider them as much an individual as you or I.

So, to create this section I am going to provide a case study of some of the children I have worked with and how we supported them (I have changed their names to protect their privacy). Then along the way I have offered explanations provided by the professionals and the research carried out.

Every one of these children has been/ is an inspiration. I have loved working with them all and I sincerely hope that it is an opportunity that you too will get to experience.

"For some utterly illogical and bizarre reason, people often seem drawn to comparing autistic people with one another, as if this is in some way appropriate..." Autism & Asperger Syndrome in Children: Dr Luke Beardon.

What is autism? Autism is defined in "Autism and Asperger's in Children: Dr. Luke Beardon" as a different cognitive and sensory state – in other words those with autism are hard wired differently, which effects how they will respond to their environment. Autism can't be "cured".

This is like trying to "cure" a lefthanded person. Although in the past, this was deemed necessary.

As society has matured, this suggestion has seemed increasingly ludicrous. It is hoped that one day autism will be seen in the same way.

Teaching styles

This is something I am a strong believer in and in everything I have learned over the years it has been reinforced.
It very often isn't a case that the student is a poor learner, it is often that the teacher is poor at passing on their information and knowledge.

If the student isn't gaining from their lessons, the teacher/ educator will need to tweak what they do. Very often a small tweak will make an enormous impact.

Success will vary from person-to-person. Be careful when asking what the chances of success are for an autistic student.

In every person across the world their definition of success will vary. For some people, nothing less than 100% in a test is deemed a success.

For others, reaching the pass mark is a success. For some people, just surviving the day is an achievement.

We all have very different aspirations and interpretations of what success is. But what can be assumed is, the better the person's understanding, the higher their chances of success.

"Fall down 7 times get up 8" Naoki Higashida P30 "People with autism might need more time, but as we grow there are countless things that we can learn how to do, so even if you can't see your efforts bear fruit, please don't quit... Some kinds of success can be won by, and only by, sheer effort and sweat."

Be sensible with goals.

It is never sensible to set goals which are too far beyond what a student can achieve.
Again, I am a firm believer in starting just below a child's current level of ability. This way you can show them that they are capable, boost confidence and get the momentum flowing so that you can move on.
However, if you set targets which are too low, people will lose interest. Plodding is never an inspiration.

Do not ask the child you are working with to plod, just make sure you are giving them a gentle push and a guiding hand so that you are there to catch them when they stumble.

Links to other learning difficulties:
Autism is often linked to other learning difficulties. It can often be because of these other difficulties that the autism diagnoses are identified.

The connection most commonly connected is ADHD (attention deficit hyperactivity disorder). This is a problem with maintaining attention, impulsivity, and hyperactivity. Sometimes these issues stem from stress and anxiety rather than actual ADHD, especially in new social situations where they find they can't sit still and relax.

One girl I worked with briefly found analysing texts difficult as she found it nearly impossible to "stand in someone else's shoes". She could see that someone was crying but wouldn't comprehend that this meant they were upset about something.

The prospect of analysing why an author used certain language to describe/ write something was just completely out of her grasp.

Using the environment to reflect someone's feelings was also totally beyond her comprehension. Things were to an extent seen on a very superficial level.

We spent time looking at colours and their associations. The weather and what it might imply. This was done through considering films as well as text so that we had a visual image to consider. We also judged when different colours were used in the environment (red – warning signs, etc).
We kept these as mind maps and flash cards so that we could refer to them when we were writing.

I hope the following section will give you an idea that people can't be defined by their label, because no matter the label, every child will be an exclusive individual.

Every child will be different and have their own unique personality. The key thing to remember, is that these children have their own strengths and weaknesses. Their own interests and quirks. Think about them as individuals like you would any other child that you know.

Robert

I met Robert about 18 months ago. He was 19 at the time and was resitting his GCSE Maths and English. We spend an hour a week working on each subject. One of the key things that makes Robert stand out is that he takes everything very literally.
During one of the first lessons, I found this out much to my detriment.
We were looking at equivalent fractions. I used the example: Imagine there is a cake that has been cut into 4 pieces. However, 4 more visitors turn up so we're going to cut each of those initial 4 pieces in half so that we have eight identically sized pieces of cake.

In my mind this was the perfect way to explain what I meant. However, Robert seemed to bypass the logic with the fractions and focus upon the fact that if you cut the cake too small it will crumble.

No matter how I tried to divert his attention back to fractions, his only focus lay with the concern that the cake might crumble.
One of the more familiar effects of Asperger's is a tendency to make a literal interpretation of what someone says...

Another example of making a literal interpretation was that of a child with Asperger's syndrome who had completed his homework essay. His mother was bewildered as to why at the end of the essay he had drawn pictures.

He explained that the teacher had told him that at the end of the essay he must draw his own conclusions. (The complete Guide to Asperger's Syndrome; Tony Atwood, page 115.)

Although I have always offered Robert a range of resources he has nearly always opted for the more traditional form of learning. He appears to prefer a focus on structured worksheets.

When his hour's changed at college, we started doing two consecutive hours. He will normally focus well for the first hour when we are doing maths, however, when we move onto English he becomes more easily distracted. He will ask to go and get a drink of water. He will then return several minutes later with crumbs around his mouth. This happens most weeks.

However, this simple act seems to relax him. Prior to going to get a "drink" he starts rocking. "Criterion B in the DSM-IV diagnostic criteria for Asperger's Syndrome describes the characteristics of special interests that are used to confirm a diagnosis: Restricted, repetitive, and stereotypical patterns of behaviour, interests, and activities, as manifested by at least one of the following:

1. Encompassing preoccupation with one or more stereotyped and restricted patterns of interest that is abnormal either in intensity or focus.

2. Apparently inflexible adherence to specific, non-functional routines or rituals.

3. Stereotyped and repetitive motor

mannerisms (eg. Hand or finger flapping or twisting, or complex whole-body movements)

4. Persistent preoccupation with parts of objects. (APA 2000, p.84) The complete Guide to Asperger's Syndrome; Tony Atwood, page 173

Matthew

I knew Matthew for a couple of years prior to him sitting his GCSE's.
He is both dyslexic and on the Autistic Spectrum.

He always came across as quiet. He rarely wrote down any working out when doing maths though he could work out the answers, instinctively, and quite quickly.
He sat his GCSE maths 3 times before he was able to pass. Each time missing the pass by just 1 or 2 marks.
I would ask him to write everything down as if I didn't know anything and he had to explain it to me. By writing answers to an excess, I hoped that when he was left to his own devises he would fall into middle ground and write enough to get the required marks.

"Many tests and exams seem to me to ascertain, at least to some degree, the ability of the child to respond to that test or exam – and not, as the test or exam may purport, the skill level of the child in that subject area. ... He answered every single question correctly – and yet 'scored' relatively low marks. The reason for this was that the exam was marked in a certain way, including the allocation of marks for 'showing the working out'" Autism & Asperger Syndrome in Children: Dr Luke Beardon, page 100.

Simon

Simon is one of the nicest children I work with! When I first started going to him. He was about 4 ½ years old and is probably the child with the least verbal communication skills that I support.

The goal was to support him with his speech and his phonics. Though every week that I went his mum added something else that she wanted us to focus on.

The first week that I went, he curled into the corner of the settee and cried. He refused to participate no matter how much his mum tried to coax him out.

"When I fight the demands of my fixations, and when my urge to do what my fixation dictates and my determination to ignore it smash into each other, I can erupt into anger. I can erupt into anger... I want to take control of the situation, but my brain won't let me.... My rage is directed at my brain, so without thinking anything through, I set about punching my own head... The more frantic and desperate I become, the more I punch myself: by now, it's no longer about punishing my brain, it's about punishing myself..." Fall down 7times, get up 8. Naoki Higashida p.185/6

Week 2 started off pretty much the same way. By the end of the hour, we were sat at the same table, and he was intrigued by the various games I had with me. From here we started to make progress.

Our initial weeks would involve focusing on one sound.

So, the first week we focused on the 'A' sound. We had a piece of paper that had had a large letter 'A' and a range of pictures of things (nouns) that could be coloured in.

Examples would include an ant, apple, arm, anchor, etc. We would talk about what we were colouring, the colours we were using and the sound that the word began with.

We would also order the letters in the alphabet and try to make various words that started with that sound. It quickly became apparent that he was very good at sounding out words to spell them.

Having established this we then moved on to writing the words next to the images that we coloured.

Then we progressed again so that we had to fill the missing word (that matched the image we were colouring) into a sentence.
However, the sentences didn't sit next to the correct image, so we had to colour, cut, and write.

These days we are focusing on the times tables.

He likes routine and things he is familiar with. So, I take an image with me to colour. Each part of the image has a multiplication question focusing on our specific times table. Once answered correctly, that part of the picture can be coloured in accordingly.

(We normally use a Paw Patrol picture downloaded from Google as this relates to one of his passions). We will also play various other times tables games, suggestions for which can be found over in the Clara James Approach, membership group.

The games are intended to create the different memories and ensure we don't get too stuck in a rut with one specific activity style.

When he wins, he is one of the happiest children I know.

He stands up, runs on the spot waving his arms in the air and cheering.
If I win (which I rarely do as he is inclined to cheat) I am expected to do the same.
If we draw, we do a high-five before we celebrate.

"Routines that are implemented ... ensure greater predictability and certainty in life. The person develops a cataloguing or ordering system based ... that is reassuring and calming. People with Asperger's Syndrome often have a difficulty establishing and coping with the changing patterns and expectations in daily life." The complete Guide to Asperger's Syndrome; Tony Atwood, page 185.

Harry

Harry is another lovely lad.
He was not diagnosed until he reached secondary school. When his mum said that they were getting him tested it wasn't really a surprise.

He would get up halfway through the lesson and wonder off to do something that had suddenly occurred to him.

When we went into lock down and we started doing online lessons, they often proved interesting.

I'd message them a couple of minutes before the lesson and say I'm ready when they are. He'd reply and ask if he can have a minute. He then vanishes for half an hour to play with their puppy. He has no concept of time.
One lesson he explained to me how he had emptied his three pencil cases onto the windowsill and lined everything up in an organised manner.

The teacher had asked who the pencil cases belonged to. He had seemed bemused that she had questioned that he had so many pencil cases and had organised the contents in such a fashion along the windowsill.

"About 25 per cent of adults with Asperger's Syndrome also have the clear clinical signs of Obsessive Compulsive Disorder... This can include ensuring that objects are in line or symmetrical, hoarding and counting items or having a ritual that must be completed before the child can fall asleep." The complete Guide to Asperger's Syndrome; Tony Atwood, page 138.

Harry enjoys maths but his true passion lays in coding and technology. On one occasion when I arrived, he showed me a light he had created with his dad that could be activated by an app he had created for his phone. I was gob-smacked, he seemed to think it was an everyday achievement!

Chris

When I first met Chris, he had just sat his GCSE mocks and had got a U. He had failed to get any marks on any of the three papers. When I arrived each week, everything would be laid out on the table ready for us.

One of his biggest hurdles seemed to be his confidence. We went back to basics on everything.

Again, very often his preference was to do formal worksheets (though the final few minutes of the lesson would be spent playing pairs or times tables noughts and crosses).
But part of going back to basics also involved reinforcing that he needed to write down his working out and specifically what he needed to write.

If you didn't tell him, he wouldn't write down anything, including the answer. He might verbally tell you the answer but wouldn't think about writing it down.

"Children will range from being non-verbal to verbose. ... A verbal child may have more anxiety related to speech as there will be higher expectations for her to use it, despite the fact that PNT language can be highly baffling and, therefore, anxiety inducing!

Teacher: Class, time to finish.
Teacher: Jane, I've told you to finish!
Jane: No, you didn't, my name isn't 'class'
Teacher: Don't be so cheeky, you'll get into trouble! Jane ends the school day wondering, yet again, why being so accurate with language has got her into trouble..."

Ed

I knew Ed for a few years before I started working with him. I worked with his older sister first and was then asked to spend some time with him after she finished her GCSE's.
Before we started, I was told they were like chalk and cheese. This is very true. Ed struggles when he comes across something new.

He needs to organise everything before we can start.

He struggles at school with making friends and has been the victim of bullying several times. Unsurprisingly, Ed was recently diagnosed with Autism.

We try and help by always starting just below his comfort zone, then build up from there. One of our biggest objectives is to try and boost his confidence.

The lessons need to be fun and varied so that he is willing to participate and not put barriers up.

Consequently, when possible we adapt any worksheets into games; the board game, pairs or noughts and crosses are most common. With confidence we will hopefully be able to create a self -fulfilling prophecy. He will be willing to have a go and from there he will get better, and the spiral of success will start to grow.

"People with Asperger's Syndrome are often perfectionists, tend to be exceptionally good at noticing mistakes and have a conspicuous fear of failure.

There can be a relative lack of optimism, with a tendency to expect failure and not to be able to control events (Barnhill and Smith Myles 2001) The complete Guide to Asperger's Syndrome; Tony Atwood, page 141

Tim

Tim is different to the other children I have worked with. The others have all been high functioning, whereas Tim would walk/bounce/dance around smacking his chest and had very limited vocabulary.
I worked with him in a residential unit.

He was 16.

Very often during his bath time he would sing nursery rhymes to himself. Water was his love and trying to persuade him that he needed to get out of the bath because the water was cold, was no mean feat.

The residential unit was for children who couldn't function in a mainstream school. This might be for many reasons: sensory overload with all the movement, noise, or people.

Many of the children there also had other underlying conditions such as ADHD and asking them to sit in a room full of people would have been too much for them to cope with.

Sadie

Sadie is great. She's 10, in year 5 at primary school. Her brothers are both on the autism spectrum and she has told me that she might be as well.

She struggles socially and finds it hard to make friends at school. Her parents got in touch to ask for help with the 11+. They felt that if she could get into a grammar school where the class sizes were smaller, she might cope better.

She is a very logical thinker. Sadie appears to find maths and verbal reasoning a straight - forward thought process. Her memory is also particularly good at recalling spellings.

One time she told me they had been to church in the morning. After the service there are drinks and biscuits for the congregation. Her brother had been spotted going for, what the lady behind the counter had thought to be his second biscuit.

She told him that he would be welcome to take another if he told her how many he had already had.

I think she felt his conscience would make him feel bad about taking another. Instead, he declared, this was his 4th. He took the biscuit, said thank you and set about eating it.

I had to smile to myself at this story. "Children with Asperger's syndrome are brutally honest and speak their mind. Their allegiance is to the truth, not people's feelings. They may have to learn not to tell the truth all the time...

Children with Asperger's may benefit from Social Stories ™ to understand why it is appropriate at times to say something that is not the truth, and when to stay quiet." The complete Guide to Asperger's Syndrome; Tony Atwood, page 77

Suggested additional reading.

During this section I have referred to Tony Atwood's: The Complete Guide to Asperger's Syndrome.

It has been insightful and inspiring whilst writing this section.

Before writing I did a lot of background research. Some of the books felt like reading a university textbook, these are two I would like to recommend to you now:

"My son is not Rainman" The story of living with a son who is diagnosed as having autism. It's insightful from the perspective of a parent.

As a book it also an emotional read which will have you in tears and laughter. I recognise that sounds corny but it's the most honest way I can find to describe it.

"Can you please. sit. still!"

For some children, the answer will simply be 'no'. This was something I learned a while back. For some children the concentration it takes to sit still, don't fidget, don't do anything, just sit still, is like a super-power in itself.

It has been estimated that approximately 11% of children have been diagnosed as having ADHD. Children who are:
· Easily distracted and consequently have trouble focusing and concentrating.
· Become quickly exhausted when they have to apply themselves mentally.
· Loud!
· Impatient and cannot wait...

Studies have revealed that ADHD could be the result of the child having less grey matter in their brain. Also, the areas responsible for impulsive behaviour, emotional regulation and short-term memory may be wired differently.

If this is the case, what it doesn't affect is their intelligence. Often the brains of children with ADHD will mature later.

There are 3 main types of ADHD.

The inattentive type.

This version often results in the child being easily distracted and struggles to pay attention. They get easily bored which makes it hard for them to focus. As a result, it means that your child may often miss the important detail of what is being said. They lose things and it often takes a while to process the information that they are given, possibly because they've missed key parts of it.
They live in a world that is packed full of daydreams. I suspect most of us would like to exist somewhere like this!

As parents when we are working with children who are less organised and loose things, I would suggest that we share the responsibility of making sure we have everything needed for what we are going to be doing. Maybe it's by reminding them in advance what we are going to need, written, or spoken. Double checking it's all to hand before you start.

If it's not, don't worry just spend the two seconds that will be needed to grab it and highlight that next time you will both need to be extra sure that it's not forgotten.

If a fuss is made this early on, the rest of what you want to do will be set on rocky foundations.

Although you will be working on one specific theme, you will possibly choose to divide this into multiple smaller, interactive tasks so that there is a quicker turn around and concentration is not needed for so long.

Allow them to choose which task is done next when possible and make them varied. This is certainly a time when a selection of worksheets probably won't be appropriate.

Reward good concentration, and if you notice it's slowly waning, have a break for a minute or two, grab a drink or something and then come back to what you were doing.

When you're explaining something, keep it brief. One step at a time. Maybe, if possible, back it up with visual images (an older child may want to create them themselves, they can always then be kept for revision purposes when the time is needed) or as written instructions. If you use words, also use colour.

Hyperactive Impulsive Type

Children which are recognised as having this type of ADHD will have an inability to sit still and control their impulses. Unfairly they are often labelled as "naughty' or 'busy' as they instinctively respond to every stimulant around them.

- They struggle with social skills.
- The desire to touch and play with everything within reach is too great to resist even when told not to.
- Talking seems to be a reflex, something that never ceases.
- They can't wait their turn and often blurt out the answers even when they've been asked not to.
- Without thinking about the consequences of their actions, they will often act impulsively and without thinking.

If your child has the hyperactive Impulsive Type of ADHD I would suggest, and this at times will be hard, the most important thing you can do is be patient.
If they find walking and thinking easier, let them do it.

Perhaps sitting at a formal desk or table isn't the most practical option for your child.

Although it is what is commonly suggested as there may be fewer distractions, the act of sitting still in itself may be enough that your child can't focus on anything else.

Talk to them, ask them what they find the easiest. What do they feel is the most productive. It may be that at times, it is the most beneficial if they talk and you write rather than expecting them to form the written answer.

Plan their work, start with a brain dump. You may choose to cut the ideas out and then place/stick them down in the order you choose to write about them.

Make it physical and interactive.

Like I say, talk to them about what works best as they know themselves better than anyone else does.

Diagnosis will need to be carried out by your doctor. But getting your child diagnosed is important. A child with ADHD may be disruptive in class and struggle to keep their emotions under control. These children may be unfairly labelled as 'naughty' or 'weird'.

It is likely they will get behind with their schoolwork and eventually become unable to catch up. They may see themselves as different and therefore be socially awkward making them feel lonely and isolated.

Around 50 percent of people with ADHD also 'suffer' from other conditions such as:

· Depression
· anxiety disorders
· OCD - obsessive compulsive disorder
· ODD - oppositional defiant disorder
· learning difficulties
· tic disorders

They may also experience extreme anxiety, being in constant trouble in class for not behaving.

'Cortical wiring' refers to the structure of the cerebral cortex in the brain. It is the cerebral cortex which is responsible for further high-level brain function, such as reasoning, reading, and writing.
Therefore, challenges with this may include learning disabilities or difficulties such as:
* Dyslexia or dysgraphia,
* Language disabilities
* Struggling with fine motor skills, like writing
* Gross motor skills such as running, jumping, or catching a ball.

Each of these may have consequences with their academic attainment. Making them feel as if they are sick or naughty or stupid. Talk to your child in a positive way about ADHD and share stories of them of celebrities and other successful people who have use their ADHD to their benefit.

Acknowledge living with ADHD can be challenging at times, and the fact that they may be labelled as naughty, annoying, or weird, is not fair. Reassure them that you're always there to talk to them, to listen to them, assure them.

It's our responsibility to try and support their self-esteem, to reassure them that you love them then that you're on their side.

There will be times when you need to make compromises and lower your expectations and remind yourself that your child's behaviour is not caused intentionally, it is a consequence of their ADHD.

The combined type

This is the type that most people with ADHD display. This means that they show signs of both hyperactivity with a compromised impulse control, whilst at the same time struggle with concentrating and processing information.

You will need to accept that your child functions differently from other children. Never compare them, we are all individuals regardless of whether we have a label or not.

It may help by implementing a daily schedule, ensure you incorporate into this enough sleep and exercise.

Support them in planning their day and week so that they can predict when certain activities will take place. It will help their self-esteem if they feel that they are in control of their lives, which in turn will make them feel better about themselves. They may then start to believe that they can be successful.

When you're supporting them with something break it down into small bits. It may even just be one thing at a time such as "Ok, please can you open the book, and now can you turn to page 52."

Patience is key.

Homework

Homework is stressful with pretty much every child, however, homework with a child who has ADHD is even more stressful!

The need to remember due dates, instructions, be organised and planned, is a recipe for disaster.

Try and make sure your child writes down their homework whilst they are still in the lesson. If the teacher can send it to you, or give a copy to your child, that would be even more helpful. I guess that is the perk of many of the automated homework sites that schools now use.

Once their homework is done, ask them to put it in a specific place. It might be a folder, box file, bag, etc so that you can ensure things are put in the appropriate place to be taken to school on time. As parents, it is only fair that we accept some of the responsibility and help to ensure that they have it on the day that it is needed to be handed in.

.

A homework 'to-be-done' pile is probably even more important, especially if you can attach a post-stick note to it, stating the date it is due by. If it is set by the class teachers online, ask for the password so that you can access the portal as well, or just have a daily check in their homework diary if they have one. Checking what is needed to be done and when by.

Try and set up a homework routine. Some children would rather get it over and done with as soon as they get home from school. Others would rather get changed, have something to eat and drink, relax first.

What works best for your child? Again, talk to them about it. They know themselves best and what they will find most manageable. If you can have an allocated place for doing homework with as few distractions as possible. It may not be a desk, it may just be somewhere where they feel relaxed, the lighting works and people won't be talking and passing by.

Make sure they have everything that they need. It may be worth creating a box which stores everything they might need for homework.

If the items in here are additional to the ones they take to school, that would be better as they may get forgotten if they are not put straight back into their bags.

The box may hold pens, pencils, scissors, a calculator, highlighter, rubber, ruler, etc. Equally important is that you help them to manage their time, encourage them to take regular breaks. The concentration needed takes a lot of effort, it will be exhausting. Don't expect them to slog over something for hours. Sometimes, short sharp bursts are more beneficial.

If they become too exhausted, allow them to stop. Try again another day. Speaking to one mum once, she said to me that it wasn't worth the argument. At the end of the day her relationship with her son was too important to her. We are here to support our children. If we push too hard there is always the risk, they will fall.
Offer support, love, and guidance.
Look after their self-esteem and make sure that their teachers are educated on ADHD and your child in particular. Every child is an individual, even if they have the same

learning difficulty as someone else who the teacher has previously worked with, they are individuals and will have their own needs, and requirements.

Being a parent of a child with ADHD is challenge. There will be times when you want to scream, to cry, to pull your hair out, but try and stay positive. Try and find the good in everything. Try and maintain a sense of humour.

Life is generally easier when you smile and often, when we do, our brain concludes we are genuinely happy and as such we start to believe it ourselves.

As a parent try and provide structure, routine and a predictable environment, life will be much easier for them. In turn, it will also be easier for you.

Try and reward instead of shouting, even if what can be praised seems insignificant, focus on it and be proud of it. Remember, even though sometimes it will be hard, it's not always their fault.
Find the things your child is good at and encourage them, embrace them, find an opportunity to do it more.

It's not fair to punish things that they can't control. I started this section with the commonly used term: 'can you please sit still?' Fidgeting, not finishing something, getting distracted, is not their fault. Let it go, try not to get too hung up and the small stuff that can't be changed.

Often it may be our fault because we haven't explained something clearly enough. Keep it short, keep it simple and ask them if they get it. Maybe even ask them to explain it back to you.

Homework is stressful, and often this stress will unwittingly be responded to in a fight or flight response. Keep it calm. Give them a break, take one yourself if needed. This is key. Look after yourself as well.

Many of the suggestions made in the dyslexia section will also work for children with ADHD. Keep it engaging, make it fun, offer multiple learning resources, ensure they understand, and you are explaining it in a way that is relevant.

Maybe this section doesn't belong in this book as in itself anxiety is not a learning difficulty. However, anxiety is so closely attached to everything I have mentioned prior to this section it seemed wrong not to include it.

Anxiety can be brought on by so many different things, maybe it's the by-effect of the stresses caused by dyslexia, ASD, ADHD. Or maybe it is something completely different; the death of someone, a change of circumstances, the fear of failure, not being up to the standard of their peers, the concern created by the fear that they won't fit in. The list is endless.

But I feel that everything I have said prior to this, holds true here. It is our responsibility as parents to support our children. To try and boost their confidence, to show them love. When we are working with our children it is important to recognise their body language as often more is portrayed through what is not said rather than what is said. Like a chameleon we need to act accordingly. We need to recognise when to be excited and outwardly enjoying the experience, and when to quieten down and be calm and reassuring.

Be aware that moving onto something new or something slightly harder may cause some children to worry. Start just below their level of comfort to reassure them that they are capable, they can do it. You have every faith in them. Then once they are confident with the basics move on from there. Never try to, metaphorically speaking, jump in at the deep end to establish if they can swim.

If they seem scared or anxious at all ask them if they want to tell you what's worrying them. If you have a pet, they may prefer to talk to the pet. Pets will never judge or repeat what we say. If not, they may like to write it down then get rid of it after. Sometimes once something is said, the problem never seems so big.

If they do open up to you, don't judge. Listen quietly and always reassure them that you love them and will do anything that you can to help them.

If the anxiety is building, suggest taking a break. Ask them if they would like to get some fresh air for a moment. Perhaps suggest they get a drink so that you can provide a distraction and give them the opportunity of some alone time.

Never force the conversation. If what you were planning on working on isn't going to be practical today, don't worry there's always tomorrow. Grab something else and refocus. I was speaking to a mum recently and she was telling me about the battles she sometimes faced with her son and like she said, very often these things aren't worth arguing over. At the end of the day, their relationship is so much more important than anything else.

Savour today and the time that you have together, make it quality time.

Final notes:

I hope you have found the points in this book helpful. I would love to hear your feedback. If you have questions or comments, please do get in touch with me at info@clarajamestutoring.co.uk, or leave a review on Amazon.

I promise I will always do my best to help. Throughout the book I have mentioned the Clara James Approach, the membership group I created back at the end of 2022. Each month a new bundle of resources is added and although they are not designed specifically for children who display different learning styles, I have used them consistently over the past 11+ years since I started Clara James Tutoring, very often with children who learn differently to the mainstream. There is also a Facebook group where you can speak to other parents and a monthly zoom call where you can ask questions about your child's maths or English and I will support you the best I can.

The membership is supposed to be £12.95/month, however as a thank you for reading this book I shall offer you an annual subscription of **just £7.95 for the year** with all the profits going to charity. For more information about the group visit:

https://theclarajamesapproach.co.uk/cja-info-page-8341

I will no doubt finish this conclusion then remember things I should have added, so follow me on Facebook ((11) Clara James Tutoring | Aylesbury | Facebook) or get in touch and ask to join our fortnightly newsletter and those things I forgot to put in the book, I will mention there.

Once again, thank you for taking the time to read this book. I hope you have found it helpful and good luck to both you and your child.

Warmest wishes, Dawn

About the author

Like so many women I ended up working in education and child-care because it fitted in with a young family.

I had an amazing childhood. The youngest of two, though throughout school it was often brought to my attention that I wasn't as clever as my brother. As an adult, I've learned to accept the fact that very few people are.

I was married at 19, then Clara was born just before my 21st birthday. Jamie came along 17 months later, then almost 2 years to the day later, our youngest, Angel was born.

At 24 I decided to do something more with my life. Dad had died just as I started my A' levels and my academic dreams vanished at that point. But after a holiday back to the town where I was brought up, I realised it was time for a change.

Initially, I went into the playgroup which Clara attended and asked if I could work there as a volunteer whilst I studied for my diploma in preschool practice.

Within a couple of months, I was offered the paid role of SENCo (Special Educational Needs Co-ordinator) and was asked to also assist with the planning, policies, and procedures for the setting.

Over the coming years, I completed the diploma. Then I continued and did a degree in childcare and education through the Open University.

As my daughter started junior school, I questioned whether she might be slightly dyslexic. Verbally she was very astute, but her spelling was dreadful and her interest in reading; non-existent.

The school instantly dismissed the idea. They told me that dyslexia was an excuse for laziness so I didn't have anything to worry about. At the time I didn't have the confidence to fight my corner. So, I decided that if they wouldn't help her, I would do what I could to help her myself.

Over the coming years I finished my degree and also studied numerous other courses on learning styles, learning difficulties and anything I could get my hands on.

I worked in mainstream schools, creches, a residential unit for children with profound autism that couldn't cope in mainstream schools. In addition, I worked as an NVQ assessor in early years and as a childminder.

One of the main things that became apparent was that we are all different. We all learn differently. Additionally, it is far harder to embrace what we are being taught if we are not relaxed and open to learning.

Furthermore: if we do something once, we create a memory. So, for example, if we do a worksheet, that information is lodged somewhere in our mind. If we complete a second worksheet, we are reinforcing that knowledge. But our brain still only has one place to go to find the information that it needs.

However, if we do a range of different activities, we are creating more memories within our brain. When that information is needed, our brain has more places to go to where it can find the knowledge that it is seeking.

Whilst on one course, a friend suggested that I had a go at tutoring. At first my idea was that it would be nothing more than to complement my other job.

I wasn't sure what was expected of a tutor, even though by this stage I had about 12 years' experience working in education. So, another friend and I brainstormed what we would expect from a tutor.

When I started Clara James Tutoring in 2012, it was based on the following values:
Lessons needed to be varied, enjoyable, relevant.

We are all individual and learn differently, and As a parent what would I expect from a tutor?

Clara is my oldest daughter; Jamie is my son. The logo is an angel holding a book, Angel is my youngest daughter.

I hoped by offering a personal name it will reflect the personal service we deliver and demonstrate we are not a generic brand.

We quickly proved to be different to most other tutoring platforms, but I think that is largely why we have done so well. We haven't followed the masses; instead, we followed our hearts and our conscience. Everyone is there to be helped. They want to feel important, and they didn't just get in touch to make our bottom line (profits) grow.

Now we not only offer 1 to 1 tutoring in the student's home and online, but we also have a range of mini courses, the SEN training course which compliments this book will be coming soon, and we have the membership group (the Clara James Approach) offering resources for parents to use themselves at home.

In addition, we offer help in becoming a tutor through the Clara James Brand Associate Opportunity, Clara James Tutoring Franchise and one to one mentoring.

Life hasn't taken the route I expected, but working with so many amazing children over the years has brought me so much happiness. There have been times of frustration, times for tears of joy.
Would I change it? No chance.
Thank you for reading to the end of this book. Warmest wishes,
Dawn

Printed in Great Britain
by Amazon

22597747R00106